D1216603

Towards a Curriculum for All

A practical guide for developing
an inclusive curriculum for pupils attaining
significantly below age-related expectations

Dorchester Curriculum Group

David Fulton Publishers
London

David Fulton Publishers Ltd
Ormond House, 26–27 Boswell Street, London WC1N 3JZ
www.fultonpublishers.co.uk

First published in Great Britain in 2002 by David Fulton Publishers

Note: The right of The Dorchester Curriculum Group to be identified as
the authors of this work has been asserted by them in accordance with
the Copyright, Designs and Patents Act 1988.

Copyright © 2002 The Dorchester Curriculum Group

British Library Cataloguing in Publication Data
A catalogue record for this book is available from the British Library

ISBN 1–85346–773–1

Typeset by Textype Typesetters, Cambridge
Printed in Great Britain by Bell and Bain Ltd, Glasgow

Contents

Contributor profiles

Dede Bourne is Deputy Headteacher at Langside School in Poole. She is a trained psychologist and teacher with a masters degree in Special Education from Exeter University. She has worked with PMLD pupils for many years at home and abroad.

Diane Chadwick is Early Years Co-ordinator and Reception/Nursery teacher at Yewstock School in Dorset. She was awarded a BEd (Hons) in Special Education at University of Northumbria and has over sixteen years' experience of working with pupils with SEN, including nine years teaching reception and nursery-aged pupils who experience SLD/PMLD.

Margaret Fewtrell is teacher-in-charge of the PMLD resource base at Linwood School in Bournemouth. She is also Head of Department (SLD/PMLD) and has over twenty years' experience of working with pupils who experience PMLD.

Jenny Goodman is currently teacher-in-charge of the Supported Learning Class at Montacute School in Poole and has curriculum responsibility for Science throughout the school. For the past five years her teaching experience has included children with PMLD and SLD at Key Stages 1, 2 and 3.

Chris Hewlett is a teacher at Mountjoy School in Bridport, Dorset. For the past nine years she has been teaching pupils who experience PMLD and during this time has taught pupils at every Key Stage. She is also the school's subject coordinator for Science and Design Technology. Having initially trained to teach in mainstream primary schools, Chris has an Advanced Certificate in Education, specialising in SEN/PMLD.

Stephen Mason is Inclusion Co-ordinator at Linwood School in Bournemouth. He originally trained at Westhill College, University of Birmingham, and has over ten years' teaching experience working with a wide range of pupils with special educational needs. Stephen has taught classes in Key Stages 2 and 3 with an inclusive PMLD ethos.

Hilary West trained and worked for a number of years in primary schools. She undertook a DPSE course at University of the West of England specialising in teaching pupils who have SLD and PMLD. Hilary is currently English subject leader and teaching in the PMLD unit at Yewstock School (since September 2001 these pupils have been included with their peer groups).

Foreword

This essentially practical book focuses on a major challenge: that of ensuring that *all* pupils receive an appropriate curriculum that encompasses the statutory requirements of breadth and balance of the National Curriculum and also meets the individual learning needs of each pupil. In rising to the challenge, the Dorchester Curriculum Group of teachers investigate the needs of those pupils who have profound, multiple and complex learning difficulties and who are often at early stages of development and learning.

Such pupils have not always been part of the education system and until 1971 they were deemed to be 'ineducable' and were the responsibility of the Department of Health. They were often in receipt of a medical model of care and the late recognition of their ability to learn has meant that, in comparison with other pupils with special educational needs, little has been written about their particular curricular requirements. This is not to say that good practice has not been in evidence and this book helps to bring together the principles and innovative practices of the staff of many schools who are concerned with the teaching and learning of these pupils. The contents are intended to help and support staff to plan, teach and deliver an appropriate curriculum to pupils whose rates of progression through all aspects of the school's curriculum may be extremely slow and may vary from day to day.

It does, however, join a growing number of publications which help to ensure that such pupils have appropriate challenging learning opportunities and which help their staff to support them in gaining the necessary skills, knowledge and understanding to prepare them for life after school. The ideas put forward in *Towards a Curriculum for All* complement many of those embedded in the major DfEE and QCA project *Planning Teaching and Assessing the Curriculum for Pupils with Learning Difficulties*, which was made available to schools in March 2001. This is no mere accident as the Dorset Curriculum Group played a major part, along with many other schools and individual teachers, in helping and supporting the core DfEE and QCA project team to bring together the 'good practice' experiences of curriculum development available in mainstream and special schools throughout the country.

The ideas presented in the DfEE/QCA (2001) materials are intended to be used flexibly alongside every school's existing curricular documentation. With acknowledgements to these materials, the Dorchester Curriculum Group has incorporated its own examples of innovative and distinctive ways of organising and planning the curriculum and has provided illustrations of practice based on a justification of its work. For example, the DfEE/QCA materials discuss ways in which the curriculum can be organised in order to provide an appropriate balance for the range of pupils with learning difficulties, and the Dorchester Curriculum Group has provided examples of timetabled activities for the pupils with profound and multiple learning difficulties in a range of schools. Similarly, the development of skills across the curriculum (QCA 2001) is illustrated by photographs of pupils 'learning to learn'. The examples are, of course, the Group's own interpretation of the points made and are offered not as the only possible exemplars, but as a starting point for debate and discussion for all staff concerned with the teaching and learning of pupils with special educational needs. As has been stated elsewhere, it is important to note that the development of aspects of the curriculum, such as schemes of work, may vary from school to school and will be influenced not only by the ability range of the pupils, but by the resources available and the expertise and interests of the staff (Ashdown 2001).

This book has been a collaborative venture and has involved teachers from a range of different LEAs who have shared ideas, debated and discussed their policies and practices, and, consequently, have established common principles on which to base their work. Such practice is to be commended and is in line with the notion of *talking schools* (Ainscow *et al.* 1996). The members of this 'team' have helped to ensure that knowledge gained from the everyday experiences of the teaching and learning of pupils with profound and multiple learning difficulties invites further discussion in a wider arena.

Towards a Curriculum for All supports inclusive learning, and to quote the DFES (2001) Statutory Guidance on inclusive schooling, 'schools . . . should actively seek to remove the barriers to learning and participation that can hinder or exclude pupils with special educational needs' (p. 2). The Dorchester Curriculum Group has made a noteworthy contribution towards this aim and although the focus of the book is on those pupils with complex needs, it contains many ideas that are relevant for those working with a range of pupils with special educational needs. By establishing and defending the principles and priorities on which the education of their pupils is based, the 'team' has contributed to the important *processes* of developing inclusive education and, ultimately, of developing a 'curriculum for all'.

Christina Tilstone
School of Education
The University of Birmingham
November 2001

Acknowledgements

The members of the Dorchester Curriculum Group are extremely grateful to Richard Byers for all his thoughtful guidance with our work. We are also delighted that Dr Christina Tilstone has written the foreword for the book. The Group would also like to thank the SEN Advisory teams at the Boroughs of Bournemouth and Poole and Dorset Local Education Authorities for funding the original project which has led to the production of this book.

We would also like to thank our colleagues and especially the pupils from the schools in the Group without whom this book would not have been possible.

Introduction

Designing an inclusive curriculum for all pupils is not easy. The authors wish to alert readers to the developing framework of curriculum design which is moving towards a more inclusive model of curriculum entitlement. *Towards a Curriculum for All* has been written by the practising teachers of the Dorchester Curriculum Group (hereafter referred to as the Group) as a practical guide for developing an inclusive curriculum for pupils attaining significantly below age-related expectations. The Group comprises practising teachers from schools in Dorset, Bournemouth and Poole who are currently working with pupils and students who experience profound and multiple learning difficulties (PMLD).

The Dorchester Curriculum Group

The Group originally met in March 1998 as the 'Dorset Project' in response to OFSTED inspections in special schools in 1997/98. This first round of special school inspections identified many strengths in Dorset schools, but made a number of criticisms of the curricula available to pupils who experience PMLD. While it was never easy to accept such criticisms, what was most evident to schools and observers was the inherent mismatch of expectations between OFSTED inspectors and the teachers they were inspecting. What one saw as good practice another saw as an impoverished curriculum. The Dorset Project was initiated to resolve this mismatch, to clarify national guidance on the curriculum for pupils who experience PMLD and to develop an agreed set of principles on which this curriculum should be founded.

The Group is extremely grateful to Richard Byers for his sure guidance, which, through promoting the confidence and knowledge of the Group, has enabled us to continue over the past two years to challenge our initial assumptions about the curriculum for pupils who experience PMLD. The Group had at its heart a belief in curriculum entitlement for all pupils, and it has been with great interest that we have contributed to the national debate on the development of inclusion. We have looked at ways to overcome the traditional barriers to learning which limit access to a broad and balanced curriculum, while retaining a clear commitment to maintain relevance to individuals' needs. Through our work we have been able to confirm and expand upon key principles and concepts and to strengthen our understanding to the point where our document *Towards a Curriculum for All* has become an explicit statement of principles, embedded in our own practice.

Our work has resulted in this book, which offers clearly laid out ideas and objectives for learning that go beyond the National Curriculum. It incorporates a holistic approach to the development of a relevant curriculum for pupils and students who experience PMLD. The book is intended for all those working with pupils and students who experience PMLD, across a range of settings.

The book's principal aims are to help staff to:

About this
book

- enrich and enhance experiences and opportunities for pupils in general;
- provide age appropriate learning experiences and contexts for learning for pupils at each Key Stage;
- set developmentally appropriate learning targets for individual pupils;
- incorporate paramedical and therapeutic provision into an inclusive framework.

This book is a proactive contribution to the use of 'P-Scales' – the QCA/DfEE framework for assessment (QCA/DfEE 2001) and to the ongoing debates on developing meaningful learning opportunities for pupils and students who experience PMLD. In the early days of the Dorset Project a great deal of time was spent assessing and evaluating current teaching practice in the light of the strategies and vision set out in the 1996 Education Act (DFE 1996), the Green Paper *Excellence for all Children: Meeting Special Educational Needs* (DfEE 1997) and the subsequent *A Programme for Action: Meeting Special Educational Needs* (DfEE 1998a). Our discussions and ideas were founded on the need to strengthen the links between what was actually set out as guidance and principles in these papers and the reality of providing equality of learning for all our pupils with special educational needs (SEN). We began to address the issue of developing curriculum entitlement for pupils who experience PMLD by brainstorming and re-brainstorming the relative roles of education, therapy and care. The Group debated how the statutory requirements within the National Curriculum (DfEE/QCA 1999) could be met by the guidance from the School Curriculum Assessment Authority (SCAA 1996a) on planning a curriculum for pupils who experience PMLD.

In our experience, there exists a paradox in whole school curriculum design which shows that the more profound the personal and special needs of pupils are, the more likely it is that their access to a broad, balanced and relevant curriculum becomes polarised towards meeting individual need. Our work led us to the realisation that the ethos for curriculum entitlement for pupils who experience PMLD is a shared ethos for *all* pupils. We have therefore striven to collate our work into a book that highlights many of the issues concerning curriculum entitlement and life-long learning for pupils who experience PMLD.

The core text is split into four main parts, covering the areas of our discussion. Part 1 begins with our interpretation of what constitutes profound and multiple learning difficulties. It explores the nature of the difficulties experienced by pupils with PMLD and considers ways in which these pupils may be included in appropriate learning environments. The Group dedicated much time to exploring values fundamental to their work with pupils who experience PMLD, and the contrasting challenges faced both by these pupils and by members of the trans-disciplinary team responsible for helping to meet them; the resulting statements of principles and specific aims are included here.

Part 2 is concerned with how best to create opportunities for learning. It examines first of all what constitutes learning for pupils with PMLD, considering the two continua of learning and experience. It discusses the crucial importance of developing pupils' enabling, 'learning-to-learn' skills, and goes on to explore how the continuum of experience and achievement can be used to demonstrate how pupils with PMLD make progress.

In Part 3, the key structures which enable staff to construct a whole curriculum for pupils who experience PMLD are discussed – a set of structures essentially consistent with the structures supporting the whole curriculum in the mainstream of education, and therefore inclusive in principle and practice. These key structures are: time allocation and timetables, target setting, individual education plans, schemes of work and record keeping.

Practical guidance in implementing the principles embodied in the foregoing core text is offered in Part 4, with exemplar Schemes of Work in English, Maths and Science. These schemes, based on the Group's experience of teaching pupils who experience PMLD, demonstrate how the cycle of planning, review and assessment can be used effectively to facilitate not just access to, but also teaching and learning within a broad, balanced and relevant curriculum.

It is hoped that teaching staff may also find *Towards a Curriculum for All* a helpful and timely source of guidance for identifying performance management targets, and that the book may be of use in setting individual objectives for teaching staff which will ultimately be of benefit to all participants in their pupils' learning.

Part 1
Philosophy and beliefs

Chapter 1

Identifying pupils who experience PMLD

This chapter explores the nature of the difficulties experienced by pupils with PMLD.

Before offering our understanding of what it means to be a pupil who experiences PMLD, we emphasise that we consider definitions of categories or classifications of pupils to be problematic. We regard, and approach, all the pupils with whom we work as pupils first. In other words, whatever the shortcomings of the following definition, we seek, in these materials as well as in our daily practice, to interact with pupils primarily as learners and individuals, as children and as people.

That said, we acknowledge the need for a shared language. For the sake of our discussions and in order to give a sense of focus to these materials, we have borrowed and adapted the definition of profound and multiple learning difficulties used by SCAA (1996a, p. 8):

> Pupils who experience PMLD are not a homogenous group. The range of pupils we considered in preparing these materials includes pupils who may appear, in some ways, to be functioning at the earliest levels of development; to have profound intellectual impairments; and to experience complex combinations of difficulties. They may, for example, have additional physical disabilities and/or sensory impairments. Some of these pupils may be ambulant. Some may have medical or para-medical needs in addition to their learning difficulties. Some may experience temporary or permanent regression or the loss of skills, capabilities and awareness because of their medical circumstances or through degenerative conditions. Some of these pupils may also behave in ways that challenge staff, parents and other pupils or which result in their own isolation, making it difficult to involve them in positive educational experiences. Many of these pupils will rely upon some form of adult support to enable them to interact with their environment.

All of the pupils we considered in preparing these materials experience difficulties with communication. However, in some instances, the difficulties may in reality be experienced by staff, who may need to find individual ways of developing interaction with pupils and facilitating the processes of communication, (see Part 2). These learners may often require the most intense levels of staff support in order to secure access to learning experiences, progress and achievement.

The nature of the personal challenges experienced by pupils who experience PMLD means that a range of professionals – including therapists and specialised support teachers for pupils with hearing and visual impairments – should work as a team with school staff, parents and the pupils themselves, to reduce and overcome barriers to learning. These professionals are collectively referred to as the trans-disciplinary support network.

It is important that the needs of the families of pupils who experience PMLD are recognised and respected. The trans-disciplinary support network for pupils may involve a range of staff having different perspectives, such as social work, health care, therapy and education. Although ostensibly working together for the good of the pupil, often these professionals may appear to the family to be presenting conflicting information or views as to the pupil's needs or priorities. The priorities of the parents, with regard to the care and/or education of their child/student, may sometimes also be at variance with those of the professionals. It is vital therefore that staff invite and respect the views of the parents as integral to the effectiveness of the trans-disciplinary support network. Since schools can be the place where these views are discussed, they should be able to offer suitable opportunities and a quiet space in which to do so .

However, we urge caution in linking provision to pupils' 'diagnostic labels' using placement, prior placement or statements about provision as a means of assessing pupils. Just because a pupil may be labelled as experiencing PMLD, this should not limit their opportunities for learning.

There are pitfalls in the process of describing pupils as 'having PMLD' and we challenge the notion of fixed labels and separate groupings. As with descriptors of other forms of special educational need, this label should be viewed as temporary, as problematic and as subject to regular review. Although profound and multiple learning difficulties are most usually not transient phenomena, it is not helpful to treat pupils to whom this label is attached as if they have been permanently categorised. They may, for example:

- consistently gain new skills, knowledge and understanding;
- show new responses in new circumstances;
- discover or be taught new ways of communicating;

and therefore require professionals and parents to reconsider previous expectations and prognoses. We teach with the assumption that all learners can and do learn within a continuum of learning, and that lowered expectations and restricted views of pupils' potential, based upon crude classifications, are to be avoided at all costs. As such, it is possible for a pupil who has been identified as experiencing PMLD to move further along this continuum of learning.

In our experience, unless pupils have been given the opportunities for learning within an environment where staff have high expectations for pupil achievement, they cannot rise to meet challenges, because staff do not believe in their capabilities and equality of learning.

Chapter 2

Including pupils who experience PMLD

In this chapter, we consider ways in which pupils who experience PMLD may be included in the most appropriate learning environments.

Pupils who experience PMLD should not be taught in fixed, mixed-age 'special care' classes or in permanently separate groupings. For example, in order to foster effective learning and positive attitudes among staff, parents and classmates, all pupils, including those who experience PMLD, could be registered as members of a tutor group with their age peers. All pupils, again including those who experience PMLD, will benefit from wide-ranging learning encounters shared with their age peers. These shared learning experiences will need to take place in learning environments which are suitably equipped and adapted, and that have appropriate levels of support from staff with relevant expertise.

However, pupils who experience PMLD, like other learners, also require some experience of specialist learning environments and interest-specific groupings. Pupils who experience PMLD may need to work together in specialist groupings and as individuals, for varying numbers of sessions in the teaching week, in areas which are specially adapted, equipped or staffed in order to facilitate certain procedures or approaches. These areas may be resourced, for example, with:

Supported learning environments

- staff with specialist expertise, including physiotherapists and learning support staff;
- specialist equipment, including facilities for multi-sensory work; a range of information and communications technology; and resources in support of pupils' physical development;
- facilities to enable pupils to be moved safely;
- specially adapted equipment for personal hygiene routines;
- private areas for therapeutic interventions, including physio-therapy;
- storage space for large scale items of equipment such as wheelchairs, standing frames or side-lyers.

Areas like these in schools may be described as 'supported learning environments', 'support units', 'resource bases' or even classrooms! Separate and purpose-equipped facilities may be required for younger pupils and older students. Pupils who experience PMLD may begin their learning day in these environments and use them across substantial parts of the timetable, or visit such environments briefly on an occasional basis in order to gain access to certain essential procedures. The purpose of these environments is to support access and participation for pupils who experience PMLD to inclusive learning opportunities in the mainstream of the school. The boundaries of these specialist environments should therefore be permeable, allowing pupils to move flexibly between various inclusive and specialist contexts for learning.

Under these circumstances, it is essential to have a member of staff who has a clearly designated responsibility for co-ordinating the educational, paramedical and pastoral needs of pupils who experience PMLD. This co-ordinator will maintain an overview of provision for pupils who experience PMLD through involvement in both the planning, implementation and monitoring of individual education plans and the development of inclusive schemes of work. When the inclusion occurs in a special school this role may be seen as the equivalent of the SENCO and/or Inclusion Lead Teacher in a mainstream school. The co-ordinator will also organise the flexible deployment of specialist support staff so that they move between specified activities in order to provide targeted support for individual pupils or groups of pupils in specific circumstances.

A range of contexts

As well as making use of a supported learning environment on a flexible, individually targeted basis, pupils who experience PMLD should be taught in a range of different contexts. In order to meet the varied needs of pupils who experience PMLD and their peers, there should be whole school agreement to provide appropriate group and individual timetables (see Chapter 7).

It is our intention within this book to illustrate how pupils who experience PMLD can be included with their peers within a range of settings, and integral to this are the values of entitlement, empowerment and enablement.

1. *Entitlement* All pupils are entitled to equality of opportunity, and pupils who experience PMLD have just as much right to high quality shared learning experiences as other pupils. The success of these shared learning experiences will ultimately be dependent on the quality of interactions within the learning environment.
2. *Empowerment* All pupils are pupils first, and have a basic human need for realising their self-worth and raising their self-esteem through sharing success. Pupils who experience PMLD are no different and the authors suggest that inclusion for these pupils would be a process of empowerment towards greater awareness of the world around them.
3. *Enablement* All pupils have the potential to learn from quality interactive learning experiences. Inclusion for pupils who experience PMLD has the potential to enable them to access their learning environment and interact with their peers.

The creation of a whole curriculum, differentiated to include sensory and environmental elements, becomes increasingly important when planning an inclusive learning environment which values the presence and involvement of pupils who experience PMLD (see Part 3).

The *hidden* curriculum is that part of the curriculum which is not subject controlled, and which interfaces with the school's equal opportunities policy. As suggested by Brennan (1985), it involves the whole school in shared practice that allows the pupils to be valued as developing individuals, which reflects the school ethos and values through the attitudes of all staff members. It allows education to be more meaningful for the whole person extending beyond the academic into the wider range of skills and qualities needed for life beyond school.

A child-centred approach, as opposed to predominantly subject-centred teaching, allows for pupils' strengths to be celebrated and for raising their achievements. Individual education plans (IEPs) must be embedded in the curriculum planning to enable maximum pupil progress and participation. Opportunities for pupil celebration should be maximised across the whole school curriculum, and should be intrinsic and immediate as well as founded throughout the school: 'Success, progress and achievements are relative to the individual and the reward system of the school would need to reflect this' (Dessent 1987).

The identification of the skills needed for pupils who experience PMLD to develop their self-advocacy is very much integral to the hidden curriculum. For further discussion on self-advocacy and empowerment see Tilstone and Barry (1998).

The way in which the school organises its inclusive approach is a 'potent indicator of its values system' (Dessent 1987). The school needs to be clear about what model of inclusion it is using and what purpose it serves for all the pupils, not just for those pupils with the highest levels of academic achievement. The *hidden* curriculum is not always easily absorbed by children who experience PMLD, as there may be emotional and highly individual issues which will need to be made explicit and may need to be taught.

Shared ethos and approach

There is a strong consensus of opinion that the education of pupils with special educational needs is a key challenge. *A Programme for Action: Meeting Special Educational Needs* (DfEE 1998a) makes clear that although there will be a continuing role for specialist provision, special schools will also be expected to act as a source of expertise, advice and professional development. Special school staff are actively developing this role within their local education authorities and are keen to work closely with mainstream colleagues to share and benefit from good practice.

The review of the Code of Practice indicates that mainstream schools will become increasingly responsible for providing the education for pupils registered with them who have a wide range of special educational needs. Mainstream schools may therefore need to develop their own inclusive learning environments, and the specialist services offered by special schools such as those in the Group will help this development

The changing role of special schools

Chapter 3

Statement of principles

This chapter explores some of the values we hold to be fundamental to our work with pupils who experience PMLD and their families.

We feel strongly that the pupils we know and with whom we work should not, in comparison with their age peers, experience a curriculum which is separate or narrow or reduced in scope, although they may require a more tightly focused approach to learning. There may be times when pupils who experience PMLD require learning experiences of a particular quality; the individual attention of specialist professionals; or curricular provision with a characteristic emphasis. The principles we establish here about a shared framework for learning apply to these pupils in whatever context. Thus, in accordance with Section 1 of the Education Reform Act of 1988, our aim is to provide a curriculum for pupils who experience PMLD which:

- promotes the spiritual, moral, cultural, mental and physical development of pupils at the school and of society;
- prepares pupils for the opportunities, responsibilities and experiences of adult life.

Pupils should not be disapplied from the National Curriculum simply because they are said to experience PMLD. Access to a broad and balanced curriculum, mediated by high quality teaching, provides positive experiences for all pupils, including those who have regressive medical conditions.

As a group we debated and agreed a further set of principles that we hold to be fundamental to working with pupils who experience PMLD and their families. Our work illustrates a commitment to:

- valuing all pupils as learners for whom the school experience presents a powerful opportunity to establish a secure basis for learning;
- working in partnership with pupils, facilitating, enabling and valuing their perspectives and views;
- valuing the contribution that individual pupils make to the life of a school community regardless of their disabilities;
- acknowledging and taking account of the responses that pupils themselves offer in relation to their experiences;
- supporting pupils in becoming advocates for themselves;
- working in partnership with parents in order to support them in meeting their expectations for their children.

Such a commitment, cited here with reference to pupils who experience PMLD, should be no different from any other such commitments made by staff in a mainstream school for their pupils. If we are working towards a curriculum for all, then establishing and upholding shared commitments and principles is an important step towards achieving it.

All pupils, whatever their ability, are entitled to be valued as individuals in their own right, and therefore as teachers of pupils who experience PMLD we are further committed to:

- acting as advocates for the best interests of pupils;
- working in partnership with other professionals, as members of a collaborative trans-disciplinary team;
- constantly challenging established expectations and assumptions about the range of the curriculum for pupils who experience PMLD;
- constantly extending those areas of the curriculum to which pupils who experience PMLD are offered access;
- going beyond a utilitarian curriculum model to offer:
  - a wide range of curricular options;
  - the kinds of life-enhancing extra-curricular activities which other pupils seek out for themselves in the world beyond school;
- striving to provide access to continuing, lifelong learning.

Chapter 4

Specific aims

This chapter considers some of the contrasting challenges faced by pupils who experience PMLD and members of the trans-disciplinary team of staff and families who are responsible for helping to meet and resolve them.

One aspect of the Group's discussions centred on formulating a set of more specific aims for our work with pupils who experience PMLD. As these aims emerged, we noted that they often appeared to contrast with one another in ways that seemed to present specific tensions. We have accepted and celebrated this complexity by organising our ideas into pairs of related or, where appropriate, contrasting aims as follows:

- to enrich and enhance the experiences and opportunities of pupils in general;
- to promote and maintain a high quality of life for individual pupils;

- to set developmentally appropriate learning targets for individual pupils;
- to provide age appropriate learning experiences and contexts for learning for pupils at each Key Stage;

- to increase pupils' experience, awareness and understanding of their environments and of the world;
- to help pupils to anticipate, predict and affect events;

- to offer consistency of approach;
- to foster in pupils the confidence to meet, accept and enjoy the challenge of new experiences;

- to focus precisely on those areas of learning which are priorities for individual pupils;
- to provide the widest possible range of rich experiences;

- to acknowledge the probability of a need for ongoing help and support;
- to strive for independence within each pupil's own horizons;

- to encourage and respect pupil-centred communicative abilities, however subtle or idiosyncratic;
- to enable pupils to learn to interact and communicate with a variety of people in as many contexts as possible;

- to ensure that pupils' physical difficulties are alleviated to the greatest possible extent by the use of aids, equipment, adapted resources, Information and Communication Technology (ICT), specialist spaces and technological support;

- to use such equipment creatively and sympathetically in order both to maximise social interaction, personal expression and access to the curriculum, and to the community, e.g. through the use of 'passports' and talking books, and to minimise the negative effects the use of such resources can cause;

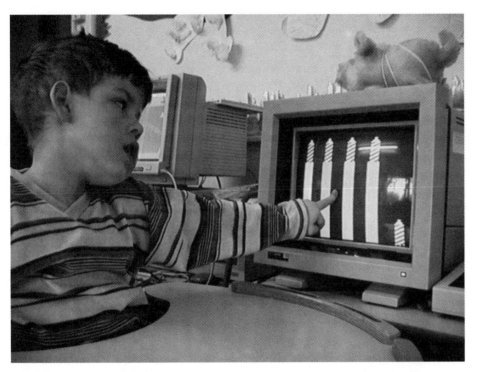

Correctly positioning a pupil (in this case a child who has left side dominance) can facilitate greater success in carrying out tasks (here, using a touch screen)

- to offer pupils the fullest possible degree of control over their own lives;
- to enable pupils to express preferences, make choices, take decisions and choose options (with negotiated boundaries) that other people respect.

The real value of these contrasting aims is their ability to suggest a framework to support planning for progression in the curriculum (see Chapter 6).

Part 2
Creating opportunities
for learning

Chapter 5
Thinking about learning

This chapter explores what might constitute learning for pupils who experience PMLD and how this can be facilitated and identified. It considers the two continua of learning and experience and offers an interpretation of what these could represent for pupils who experience PMLD.

In whatever area of the curriculum, learning for pupils who experience PMLD begins, as it does for all pupils, with *experience*. Pupils may require an extended series of apparently passive experiences in order to stimulate learning – let us say in an area of development such as problem solving. After such experiences, a pupil may become willing, or may be supported or encouraged, to become involved in learning *processes* – for example, in physical exploration or the manipulation of objects as an aspect of problem solving. As a result, some important features of this process may become established as *concepts* or areas of *understanding* – for instance, a pupil may demonstrate an understanding of the idea that a pleasurable experience results from pressing the switch for a fan to blow.

This understanding may then be developed into an area of skill or *competence,* so that the pupil may automatically repeat success, and reproduce previous accomplishments on fresh occasions. For example, under new circumstances some pupils may put into practice the ability to use a switch. If this skill can be brought to bear upon new challenges and learning opportunities as a deliberate and considered option for problem solving, then it could be said to be a learning *strategy* (such as pressing a switch to make a choice or express a preference). Pupils do not develop this strategy as part of a strict hierarchy of skills, but they will have moved along a continuum of learning which encompasses:

- experiences;
- processes;
- understanding and concepts;
- skills and competencies;
- strategy (Babbage *et al.* 1999).

Pupils do not progress in a steady and orderly fashion from experience to strategy as the weeks pass. The emerging skill that was noted last week may, for a variety of reasons, need to be reinforced with some supported participation today, and may even revert to being a passive experience tomorrow. It is also true that activities offering experiences and those facilitating opportunities to develop learning strategies need to overlap, so that pupils are constantly being given opportunities to maintain established skills as well as to engage in new processes in

A continuum of learning: how learning takes place

different areas of understanding. It is helpful to draw from this analysis a sense of the continuing importance of experiences *within* the learning continuum; and, in this sense, the curriculum for pupils who experience PMLD is no different from the curriculum for any pupil.

For many pupils who experience PMLD, experiences within the learning continuum will need to encompass a significant sensory dimension, especially to facilitate communication. This is of particular relevance when the pupils' communication environment for total communication strategies is devised. For further discussion on facilitating communication see Nind and Hewett (1994), and Coupe O'Kane and Goldbart (1998)

A pupil who experiences PMLD might learn to use a strategy (in this case, using a switch to operate a bubble tube) but the strategy itself, i.e. using the switch, needs to be taught and gained

Although the framework of the curriculum for pupils who experience PMLD should be no different from the curriculum for any pupil, it is the identification of meaningful and effective individual routes to learning, i.e. the *process*, which becomes more important. The entitlement of pupils who experience PMLD to a broad and relevant curriculum, which includes, for example, Literacy and Numeracy, needs to be balanced with an understanding that shared learning *experiences*, which may encompass a significant sensory dimension, are more relevant than the intended learning outcomes, i.e. the *product*.

Figure 5.1 gives an example of an inclusive Literacy lesson which illustrates our point that sensory routes to learning need not necessarily be solely for pupils with learning difficulties. All learners in this example are

---

(For a mixed group of pupils with moderate/severe/profound and multiple learning difficulties, involved in a themed arts week: 'Song from the Sea')

Objectives:

- To identify adjectives in shared text
- To explore the third dimension of artefacts and communicate a preference between two choices offered

Prior learning: all pupils have participated in a range of activities associated with 'Song from the Sea' which have included interactive sensory drama for pupils who experience PMLD and all pupils sharing a new song 'Song from the Sea'.

Introduction: play the song (on CD) while pupils settle into mixed-ability groups. Give each group an object of reference and a photo (sea, waves, beach) to share from a collection of sea items. Whole class to be arranged in a horseshoe format.

Lesson focus: refer to enlarged text of the song and differentiate tasks between those pupils who can

(a) read the adjectives within the text and use to expand and generate own examples
(b) use symbolised flashcards and photos to match to and share selected text
(c) explore the sensory aspects of damp and dry seaweeds, smooth and rough pebbles and shells, damp/dry sands etc., and be expected to express/communicate a preference between two items offered.

Each group to work on a range of adjectives e.g. wet/sandy/slimy/salty/windy etc. and choose a favourite to share with whole class.

Outcomes:

- Some pupils will have identified and used adjectives to expand on text from song
- Some pupils will have used symbols and/or photos to share selected text from song
- Some pupils will have explored different sensory items and expressed a preference between two offered
- All pupils will have participated in the lesson and had opportunities to share a range of learning experiences

Figure 5.1 An inclusive Year 4 Literacy lesson

being motivated by the range of stimuli offered, and the focus of the session is more on shared learning experiences than on previously identified outcomes.

Sensory work should be seen as a significant but not exclusive approach to teaching pupils who experience PMLD. In order to create a mode of access for pupils who experience PMLD it is often important to deliver lessons with a sensory dimension. This sensory dimension can on occasions be provided in a specialist environment, like a light and sound room. But sensory work is better regarded as providing a sensory route into other areas of the curriculum rather than as something separate from other subjects or areas of learning; we see it interfacing with all areas of the curriculum. **It is not appropriate to regard sensory work as the special domain of pupils who experience PMLD – apart from anything else, to do so is to deny other learners all the benefits of sensory experience in their learning, which is especially relevant when developing inclusive learning environments.**

A continuum of experience: how to recognise learning

Recognising the significance of pupils' responses to learning experiences (with acknowledgments to Brown (1996) and Byers (1996)), may take account of a range of possibilities. These possibilities may themselves constitute significant achievements for particular pupils who experience PMLD, and may usefully be recorded, assessed and reported as indicators of progress (see Chapter 11). However, the following list of responses should not be viewed as a hierarchy or as a checklist of progressive stages through which pupils will make steady progress.

Pupil responses to an activity or event may be noted in terms of:

- *encounter* – in which a pupil is present during an activity without any discernible learning outcome, although for some pupils the willingness to tolerate shared activity may, in itself, be significant;
- *awareness* – whereby staff may be able to record that a pupil has noticed, focused upon or attended to something that is going on around them;
- *response* – when signs of surprise, enjoyment, frustration or dissatisfaction can indicate early reactions worthy of note;
- *engagement* – demonstrated through smiles of recognition; interest and enthusiasm communicated through body language; focused looking or listening; attention redirected when activity shifts location; or even signs of recall when elements of the experience are repeated later;
- *participation* – characterised by sharing; turn taking; and the anticipation of familiar sequences of events, even when these aspects of involvement are supported by staff or peers;
- *involvement* – entailing active participation, with pupils striving to reach out, join in, do things or comment in some way upon the activity itself or upon the actions or responses of their peers;
- *attainment* – at which point pupils can be said to have gained, consolidated, practised or generalised skills, knowledge, concepts or understandings that related to the curricular content of their experience.

This set of ideas (adapted from Brown (1996) and with acknowledgements to Aitken & Buultjens (1992), McInnes & Treffry (1982), Uzgiris & Hunt (1975)) is intended to represent a continuum of possibility in which pupils may move around from day to day and from experience to experience. The pupil who was an active participant yesterday may, for a host of complex and hopefully temporary reasons, only encounter the experience today. Tomorrow that same pupil may attain some new skill, attitude, understanding or area of knowledge.

Responses in the continuum are illustrated in the sequence of photographs.

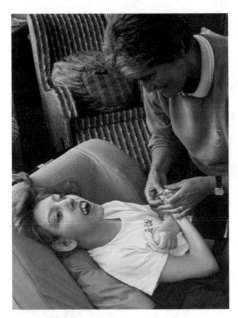

(a) Encounter

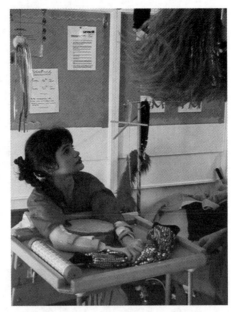

(b) Awareness

(c) Response/reaction

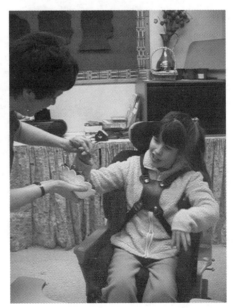

(d) Pro-active co-operation

Figure 5.2 shows how the Group have since further developed this continuum in order to show how intended learning outcomes and assessment opportunities within a holistic curriculum match the assessment framework in QCA's curriculum guidelines (QCA/DfEE 2001).

(e) Intentional participation

(f) Initiation

The continuum of experience for pupils with PMLD

In Figure 5.3, the Group offers an example of a curriculum unit of work for Science (AT 1) at KS 2, which shows how the continuum of learning might be structured with intended learning outcomes, experiences and activities, and assessment opportunities. (See Part 4 for further details on the exemplar units of work.)

The Continuum of Experience

P-Level	Intended Learning Outcome	Assessment Opportunities
P1(i)	Encounter	present/outwardly passive/reflex responses/any participation is fully prompted
P1(ii)	Awareness	affective responses/intermittent reactions/emerging awareness
P2(i)	Response/Reaction	shows interest/co-active exploration/consistent responses to familiarity (e.g. tracking, feeling, listening, looking)
P2(ii)	Pro-active co-operation	pro-active responses/communicates consistent and affective preferences/remembers and uses learned responses
P3(i)	Intentional participation	early communication responses/deliberate participation (or not)/seeks attention/sustains concentration/interested observation/explores in more complex ways
P3(ii)	Initiation	conventional communication/participates/anticipates/active exploration (physically, or with a range of senses)/turn takes

Figure 5.2 *The continuum of experience within the assessment framework (P-Levels)*

Science Key Stage 2
Attainment Target 1: Scientific Enquiry
Investigative Skills

P-Level	Intended Learning Outcomes	Experiences and Activities for Scientific Enquiry	Assessment Opportunities

3(i)	**Intentionally Participate**
	
	• with a range of multi-sensory stimuli within a scientific context
		Facilitated through activities which include the above, as well as activities which provide opportunities to . . .
		
		independently, using available senses, investigate items within their environment such as:
		
		• participate in, or deliberately choose not to participate in: group/paired activities such as; pushing balls across a table, 'playing' percussion instruments, splashing in water, stilling and listening carefully during auditory activities such as 'Sound Lotto'
		
		• act on objects in a variety of ways: crumple or pull to tear newspaper, bubble wrap, tissue paper and card; randomly squeeze and push construction equipment together; grasp and crush handfuls of cornflakes, sawdust; pull fabrics over own or adult's face or hands
		
		• search for preferred percussion instrument from a selection; search for an accidentally dropped ball; explore container after posting object into it
		
		• look at objects through visual equipment/apparatus: look at own hands or at friends' faces through a magnifying glass; look at people and faces in convex/concave mirrors; look at familiar objects through different coloured lenses
			Within a scientific context pupil may demonstrate an ability to . . . .
			
			• sustain concentration
			
			• display interested observation
			  i) focused looking
			  ii) focused listening
			  iii) reaching
			
			• communicate preverbally using physical, vocal, auditory or visual skills by:
			  i) pointing to objects or events
			  ii) searching for an object after it has disappeared
			  iii) searching for a stimulus after it has stopped
			  iv) choosing or refusing to participate
			  v) seeking attention
			
			• explore in more diverse way
			  i) rubs
			  ii) bangs
			  iii) pushes
			  iv) pulls
			  v) squeezes
			  vi) presses
			  vii) scans
			  viii) tracks

Figure 5.3 *Key Stage 2*

Chapter 6

The relationship between experience and achievement for pupils who experience PMLD

This chapter offers an interpretation of the relationship between experience and achievement for pupils who experience PMLD. It considers ways in which it may be possible to integrate key skills for learning into experiences relating to the subjects or other elements of the curriculum and to pastoral, paramedical and therapeutic provision. It then explores how the continuum of experience and achievement can be used to demonstrate how learning for pupils who experience PMLD may progress. The Group show how the curriculum for pupils who experience PMLD could be considered in terms of three broad areas of work, and how progress for such pupils can be facilitated and identified.

All teachers might offer their pupils the experience of attending concerts, visiting art galleries or watching plays while not believing that every one of their pupils will become a composer, a sculptor or a dramatist. They do, however, believe that many of their pupils may be challenged by these experiences to develop new insights into their own musical, artistic or theatrical preferences. Thus some pupils may be inspired to learn some new chords on the guitar, to take up photography as a hobby, or to watch different sorts of programmes on the television. The relationship, then, between experience and achievement is rarely direct.

Continuum of learning versus continuum of experiences

The two continua of learning and experience are perceived by some to be mutually exclusive but they are in fact interfaced with each other and we suggest that:

- learning experiences have their own intrinsic value;
- all pupils are entitled to experience a broadening range of educational encounters;
- such encounters will present pupils with new challenges.

Educators must always sustain their belief in each pupil's potential for learning so that achievement and attainment are always a possibility.

This position is far from tokenistic. Educational experiences do not have to be focused solely on immediately quantifiable attainments in order to be valid. In these terms, all pupils are entitled to become involved in a rich and varied range of educational experiences, and no pupil should be condemned to a narrow and utilitarian programme of routines simply because their potential for attainment is perceived to be limited.**This entitlement is true for any pupil and this principle should be upheld as central to a curriculum for all**.

The building blocks for the curriculum

The curriculum for pupils who experience PMLD can be considered in terms of three broad areas of work. The Group has identified these as 'building blocks' from which a broad, balanced and appropriate curriculum might be organised.

1. Key skills
2. Curriculum subjects and other elements of the curriculum
3. Pastoral, paramedical and therapeutic provision

These three broad areas of work, which we shall look at in more detail shortly, are part of an inclusive framework for the whole curriculum (OFSTED 1999; SCAA 1996a; DfEE 1999; QCA/DfEE 2001; Byers and Rose 1996; Byers 1998) which applies equally for all learners, but the balance between each area will vary according to individual need.

However, in order to promote learning within the curriculum, it is important to recognise some of the prerequisites to learning and consider how staff might create opportunities for learning and facilitate development of those 'enabling skills' that pupils who experience PMLD may need in order for learning to take place.

Creating opportunities for learning

There are specific issues for staff to be aware of in order to enable access to learning for pupils who experience PMLD. Staff need to consider how, within any of the pupil's learning environments, they can facilitate learning by:

- *developing or maintaining pupils' physical capability*, including fine and gross motor skills, co-ordination and skills in positioning, self-motivated mobility, and finding ways to enjoy and interact with the environment and the people in it;
- *encouraging pupils to actively control their environment*, including the people in it, through the expression of needs, choices, preferences or options (for example by having bright, stimulating displays and pupils' individualised items made readily accessible, such as photos of family and pets, a particular item of clothing, specific scents and sounds);
- *encouraging pupils to become more independent* or by minimising dependence in eating, drinking, dressing, personal hygiene;
- *offering contrasting experiences* that stimulate the development of pupils' awareness and communication skills;
- *giving respect for the individual pupil*, for example by allowing time for responses to manifest themselves whilst offering opportunities for joint attention, so that staff can share the pupil's focus without intrusion or interruption and are able to interpret its meaning sensitively;
- *fostering a real atmosphere for learning* and respect in the pupil's environment, for example, by ensuring that conversations between staff do not distract from the learning environment and that individual pupils are not talked *about* in their presence. Rather, that pupils should be enabled to participate in conversations as appropriate.

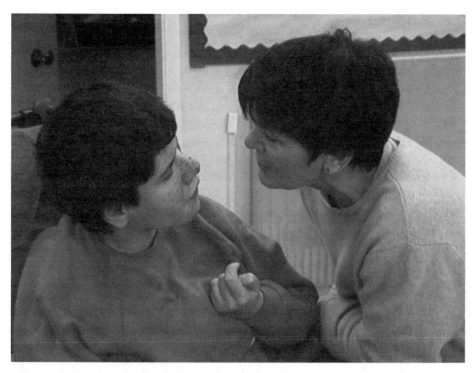

The teacher is inviting her student to engage with her without undue compromise of the student's personal space

Developing enabling skills

There are certain 'enabling skills' which pupils who experience PMLD will need to develop as their 'learning to learn' skills. A more formal representation of early developmental skills is offered in the next section on key skills. But for pupils who experience PMLD, there are many, often highly individual and personal skills and attributes which may be easily overlooked in the drive to meet curriculum standards. These enabling skills may constitute priority areas of learning for pupils who experience PMLD and will include:

- *development of communication skills*, including awareness, eye contact, turn taking, imitation, social skills, skills involved with interaction, co-operation, collaboration and working co-actively with peers and supporting adults;
- *thinking and cognitive skills*, such as prediction and anticipation, understanding cause and effect and classification of conceptual categories;
- *perceptual skills and skills in sensory awareness and exploration*, including functional use of sensory abilities and strategies compensating for or reducing the impact of sensory impairment;
- *skills in the positive self-management of behavioural difficulties*, such as responding to periods of time-out and replacing an inappropriate behaviour with a more positive behaviour;
- *developing an awareness of 'self'*, a sense of 'knowing myself', having a personal identity.

Key skills

There are a number of key skills for learning, which could be said to run through all educational experiences for all learners. National Curriculum Council (NCC 1990) and more recently the Curriculum 2000 (DfEE/QCA 1999), QCA/DfEE (2001) and the Equals/QCA conference November 2000 have defined these cross-curricular skills as 'Key Skills'. Sir Ron Dearing (1996), in his review of accreditation for sixteen to nineteen-year-olds, refined these categories into a set of key skills which, he suggested, should run through taught courses at all levels of accreditation. They are:

- *communication skills*, which may include vocalisation and speech patterns, changes in body movements and muscle tone, eye pointing, facial expressions, objects of reference, use of different augmentative communication aids (including photos, pictures, symbols, electronic communication aids, switches);
- *application of number skills*, which may include exploring and manipulating objects (e.g. to generate concept of object permanence), recognising, interpreting and predicting patterns, sequences and routines;
- *the use of information and communication technology* capability as a lifetime skill, which may include using ICT to facilitate interaction with the learning environment (e.g. using a switch to gain a specific effect) and communicating with the people in it.

We consider that these categories of key cross-curricular skills apply with just as much significance for pupils who experience PMLD as for their peers in the mainstream of education. The responses of individual pupils will vary according to the continuum we have adapted from Erica Brown's work (see Fig. 5.2, Chapter 5) and as set out in the QCA assessment guidelines *General Guidelines* (QCA/DfEE (2001)).

Dearing also suggested (1996, p. 17) that further key skills are important in 'broadening a young person's understanding of society in general, and developing personal qualities'. These key skills are set out in the QCA assessment guidelines, *Developing Skills* (QCA/DfEE (2001)) and include:

- *skills in working effectively with other people*, for example by communicating and responding appropriately when working with unfamiliar and familiar people within and beyond the classroom, such as when working with a visiting artist/musician as well as with school staff;
- *a problem-solving approach*, by using strategies to deal with challenges, for example when using an individual strategy to obtain a desired object, or when remembering how to use a switch;
- *the ability to improve own learning*, for example by indicating and responding to needs, wants, likes and dislikes, by recognising when an activity starts and finishes, and by recognising personal achievements. Pupils who experience PMLD need to be taught how to attend and/or direct their attention at a stimulus, and to sustain that attention for as long as is appropriate for the individual. These responses need to be recognised, respected and acted upon appropriately by all the adults in the pupil's learning environment; this requires the adult to be non-interventionist at times, which is an important key skill for staff working with pupils who experience PMLD.

Key skills in action: developing the concept of cause and effect

Where key skills are truly cross-curricular, they may be used to establish targets within pupils' individual education plans (see Chapter 9). Focusing on key, cross-curricular skills can help to make targets relevant to priority areas of learning for particular pupils (Byers and Rose 1996; Cavigioli 1997; DfEE 1998b). However, it is suggested as a general principle that such individual education planning targets are best addressed in the context of group activity founded in schemes of work for the subjects of the curriculum rather than in separate, individual sessions.

Where individual guidance, counselling or therapeutic sessions are required, these will constitute exceptions to this principle.

Curriculum subjects and other elements of the curriculum

Planning for subject-focused schemes of work may reflect those aspects of subjects which need to be addressed on a continuing basis, such as within mathematics sorting, classifying or making comparisons. Involving pupils in these sorts of learning processes may therefore facilitate some of the earliest forms of subject-focused achievement, and provide routes of meaningful access for pupils and students who experience PMLD to the subjects of the National Curriculum. For this reason, it is important to emphasise the subject characteristics of learning through schemes of work: pupils who experience PMLD should be taught science through a Science curriculum, and not through a PMLD curriculum. In other words, we start from the 'scienceness' of Science, as integral to the National Curriculum subject, and make this accessible for every pupil.

This will help to ensure access to a broad and balanced curriculum for pupils and students who experience PMLD and promote range, content and variety of experiences across the timetable. For example, experience and achievement in relation to the processes of sorting, classifying or making comparisons could be said to be mathematical where numbers or attributes such as shape or size are entailed. Similar skills in exploring and recognising similarities and differences, sorting and making simple comparisons, should be described as scientific where properties such as the texture, appearance or malleability of materials are involved.

In this sense, the context, the equipment or resources available, and staff awareness of the long term potential outcomes of the work, may help to define a subject focus for pupils and students who experience PMLD. This will avoid endless repetition of similar tasks that may be said to promote 'pre-requisites' for learning. Blocked units of work, focusing on the content of the different subjects and elements of the curriculum, ensure that pupils within any Key Stage engage with a broad and balanced range of learning experiences (see SCAA 1995; SCAA 1996a; Byers and Rose 1996).

In order to achieve this, the curriculum for pupils who experience PMLD should include:

- a range of sorting, classifying, comparing, ordering, pattern-making, quantifying and discriminating experiences as part of the curriculum for mathematics;
- work-related learning, sex education and health education as part of the curriculum for personal and social development;
- experiences, including simulations, relating to the recognition of similarities, contrasts and changes in time as part of the curriculum for history;
- story, poetry, role play and drama as part of the curriculum for English;
- experience of a range of information and communication

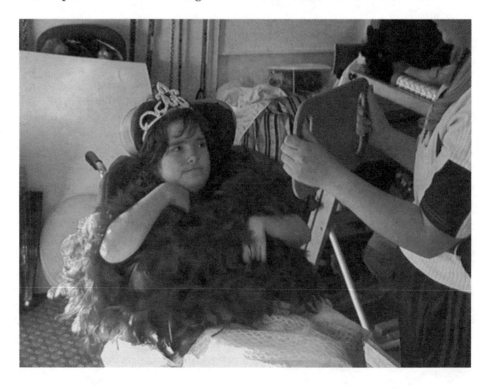

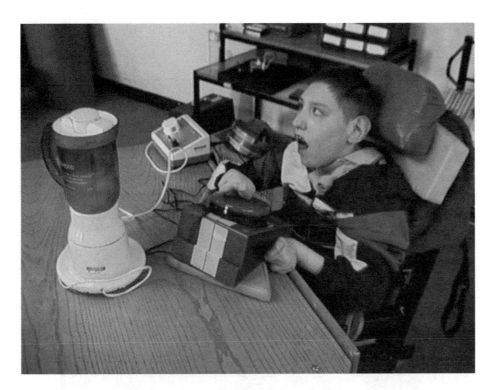

technology applications, including the uses of switch technology in communication, modifying the environment, facilitating mobility and creating effects;

- exploration of the properties and practical applications of a range of materials as part of the curriculum for design and technology, including food technology;
- access to experiences of other cultures and other peoples as part of the curriculum for modern foreign languages;
- experiences, including site visits, in relation to the recognition of similarities, contrasts and changes of place as part of the curriculum for geography;
- team games and outdoor and adventurous activities as part of the curriculum for physical education;
- creative experiences and activities as part of the curriculum for music, art, craft and design;
- experiences engendering spiritual development and awe and wonder as part of the curriculum for religious education;
- use of leisure, entertainment and relaxation facilities as part of a preparation for the role as an active citizen;
- experience of mainstream education through integration links and inclusive initiatives;
- part-time transitional links for older pupils and students with potential future placements – for example, to colleges of further education, social education centres or in the community – as part of preparation for adult life and the world of work.

● experimentation and investigations as part of the curriculum for science;

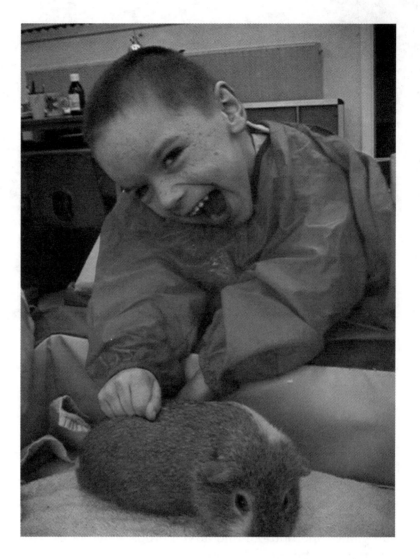

This list of suggested curriculum activities is not intended to be exhaustive nor to limit the learning opportunities for pupils who experience PMLD by offering a diminished set of curricular experiences. On the contrary, staff should be constantly striving to extend pupils' experiences into new areas. The list suggests how access to the full range of subjects can be ensured for all pupils.

This model of the curriculum encompasses all the subjects of the National Curriculum and the other cross-curricular elements which form part of the curriculum for Personal and Social Development (based on Byers 1998 and DfEE 1999). For many pupils who experience PMLD, these elements will constitute essential aspects of the whole curriculum and will demand, as a priority, resource allocation and space on the timetable. This model of the curriculum is not concerned with 'prerequisite skills' or learning for the 'developmentally young' but with those processes, concepts, understandings, skills and strategies that permeate all learning experiences. These run from the Early Learning Goals on entering education, through the Key Stages of the National

Curriculum, into the curriculum at sixteen plus, and continue on for Lifelong Learning (DfEE 1998b). For further guidelines on the curriculum for PSHE and Citizenship, see QCA/DfEE (2001).

Pastoral, paramedical and therapeutic provision

In addition to addressing key skills and curricular experiences, provision for pupils who experience PMLD will need to respond to potential pastoral, therapeutic and paramedical needs. Lacey and Lomas (1993), Lacey and Ouvry (1998) and Ware (1994; 1996) all state that pupils who experience PMLD have a wide range of needs that call for a broad and balanced (trans-disciplinary) approach by teachers and other professionals in co-operation with the pupils' parents.

Many schools therefore seek to provide:

- speech, language and communication therapy, including oral skills;
- physiotherapy, including work on physical comfort, positioning and mobility;
- occupational therapy, including work on environmental control, manual dexterity and self-feeding skills;
- support services for pupils who have visual or hearing impairments;
- support services for pupils who experience difficulties with their behaviour;
- nursing support, especially where pupils require regular medication or crisis intervention procedures;
- paramedical support, for example, in relation to eating difficulties or supported feeding such as for pupils with a gastrostomy;
- alternative therapies such as aromatherapy, massage (which are not necessarily administered by a qualified practitioner);
- hydrotherapy;
- music, art, dance and drama therapy;
- hippotherapy and/or Riding for the Disabled;
- use of an interactive sensory environment;
- access to leisure and relaxation activities;
- recreational activities (especially linked to citizenship);
- counselling and emotional support both for pupils and their families – for example, for pupils with degenerative conditions, for pupils whose parents are separating, or for pupils who have suffered a bereavement or loss of a familiar person.

Not all pupils who experience PMLD will require or be entitled to receive all these forms of support all the time. It may not be appropriate to treat elements such as these in the same way as the subjects of the curriculum, but time devoted to pastoral, paramedical and therapeutic provision should be seen as offering many important opportunities for learning. Carlton (1993) suggests that 'all therapies have a common core in aiming to develop communication skills, including attention, anticipation, turn taking, and to promote enjoyment'.

Most mainstream schools will have very limited access to the range of pastoral, paramedical and therapeutic provision as identified above, but such provision remains an important element of the curriculum for pupils with learning difficulties and will need to be sourced either from local special school or LEA resources.

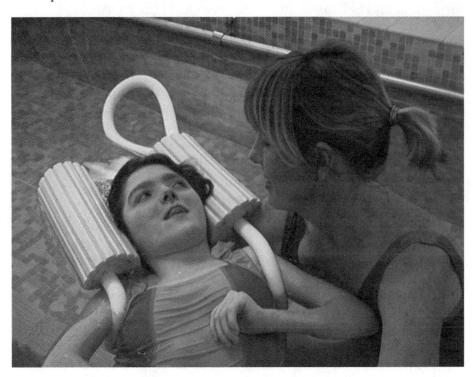

Hydrotherapy: a medium for interactive communication

The curriculum for pupils who experience PMLD, as outlined in these three building blocks (Key skills/Curriculum subjects and other elements of the curriculum/Pastoral, paramedical and therapeutic provision), may simply generate another set of headings which could then be broken down into further sets of more detailed skills. Since individual pupils will require very different, very precisely focused and very specific targets to be set in these areas, it is not useful to attempt an exhaustive step by small step analysis of each category of skill. It is, however, important to think about promoting progress in each and any of these categories across a continuum of possibility (refer to the continuum of experience as discussed in Chapter 5).

Progress for pupils who experience PMLD

Progress for pupils who experience PMLD is not a simple phenomenon. There are apparent contradictions contained in the sets of ideas below, just as there were tensions between many of our conflicting aims (see Chapter 4). Although individual pupils who experience PMLD do make progress, such progress may not be sequential and could have omissions from the recognised norms of development. We have, at one time or another, welcomed all the following outcomes as examples of significant progess for individual pupils. It is an acknowledged feature of the complexity of our work that none of these outcomes could be said to represent progress for *all* of the pupils with whom we work.

Any of the following outcomes (with acknowledgements to SCAA (1996b, p. 16), ACCAC (1999), McInnes and Treffry (1982), Aitken and Buultjens (1992)) may signal significant progress:

1. *Pupils develop meaningful communication strategies*, which might involve progress along the communication continuum from the use of concrete modes (body language, real objects and objects of reference, for example) towards the abstract (including pictures, symbols, print, signs, the use of information and communication technology and spoken words). Such strategies will increasingly enable pupils who experience PMLD to interact in meaningful ways in as wide a range of contexts as possible.

2. *Pupils develop an extending repertoire of learning positions*, thus the need to present stimuli in consistent and personalised ways (for example, close up, face to face, on the floor, with head support) is reduced.

3. *Pupils develop a range of responses* to social interactions, including resistance (which may, for some pupils on some occasions, be viewed as a positive response); tolerance and passive co-operation through supported involvement; response and co-operation towards independent activity; imitation; and pleasure in the initiation of social interactions.

4. *The frequency or severity of problem-causing and/or challenging behaviours* (such as stereotypical behaviour, extreme passivity, over-activity or activity avoidance and self injurious behaviour) is reduced, and more positive responses replace those which have become a barrier to learning.

5. *Pupils begin to generalise their responses* beyond those that are idiosyncratic and specific to certain environments, circumstances or to interactions with certain people.

6. *Pupils become able to transfer skills and concepts* they have learned from one context to another; they become able to demonstrate the same achievement on more than one occasion.

7. *The need for support* in carrying out particular tasks is reduced. Naturally, like all learners, pupils who experience PMLD will require regular opportunities to assimilate and consolidate new experiences, new skills and new understandings so that they can become confident in working more independently.

8. *Pupils begin to move on from a dependence culture* of secure and predictable routines maintained by adults, through planned choice and decision-making, towards a maximum degree of personal autonomy – characterised by risk-taking and increasing confidence in facing new experiences. Pupils are encouraged to become self-determined learners.

9. *Pupils build upon their near sense dominance* (tactile, kinaesthetic, olfactory) and start to develop increasing use of their distant senses (visual and auditory);

Using fabrics for both visual and tactile stimulation

10. *Through an assimilation of sensory reinforcement* pupils begin to acquire an increased awareness of social and intrinsic motivation.

In addition, pupils who experience PMLD are likely to need a programme of teaching the skills for alternative strategies to assist where one function become redundant, and repeated opportunities to reinforce learning across a wide range of experiences. As Fletcher-Campbell and Lee (1995) point out, some pupils may:

> ... reach a 'plateau' in their achievements – although for some pupils who experience PMLD becoming able to maintain a skill or an area of competency may in itself constitute progress; they may also experience regression – this may be a temporary situation, but in some instances can occur for the longer term or even permanently.

These phenomena are not exclusive to pupils who experience PMLD or even a characteristic of them, but they do occur. We consider that each day, and each activity, presents new opportunities for all pupils. Yet however profound or complex their difficulties may seem, these pupils are learners with the potential for making progress and engaging positively in new and familiar experiences.

Part 3
Constructing the whole curriculum

Chapter 7

Time allocation and timetables

This part of the book explores the five key structures which enable staff to construct a whole curriculum for pupils who experience PMLD: time allocation and timetables, target setting, individual education plans, schemes of work, and record keeping. This chapter discusses time allocation and timetables.

Some timetables reflect times allocated to subjects in each Key Stage, with the understanding that these proportions might be modified for individual pupils and students through their IEPs (see Appendix 2). Ideally, basic timetabling should show the range of activities and experiences offered to groups of pupils. Group and individual education plans and the allocation of staff responsibilities can then show how the class timetable is modified in order to provide specific sessions addressing the individual needs of particular pupils where these are required.

Certain aspects of a pupil's requirement for physiotherapy may need to be addressed, in part, by withdrawal from the class, whilst other aspects of physiotherapy can be incorporated into classroom activity. Personal hygiene, positioning, medical intervention, feeding strategies, therapies and physical activities demand significant allocations of time in each day. For some pupils, this could be a significant proportion of their individualised timetable, and will vary according to their needs. Beyond this allocation of time, the proportional relationships between various aspects of the National Curriculum can be maintained even if, compared with the mainstream of education, the time count in terms of hours and minutes is necessarily reduced.

There are no nationally specified times allocated to individual subjects of the curriculum (QCA/DfEE 2001). However, the core subjects of the National Curriculum require regular timetable slots while access to the remaining subjects can be provided on a rota or rolling programme basis. For example, some teachers follow a two-week timetable in order to secure this sense of proportionality. In other cases the use of a long term plan to balance time allocation over the entire year highlights the study of subjects to particular terms in a rolling programme or to indicate curricular options and/or specific modules. Although the time allocation for specific subjects is not dictated, staff are required to justify timetable balance for each individual pupil. Clearly, a timetable for a class solely for pupils who experience PMLD will differ from a timetable for an inclusive group. Examples of timetables are shown in Figures 7.1 and 7.2.

Some schools maintain separate teaching groups for pupils who experience PMLD whilst others are working towards more inclusive approaches to groupings – although a mix of setting arrangements and diverse groupings can encompass the benefits of both approaches (see

Class: Junior (KS 2/3) **Date – Term:** Autumn 2000

Time	Monday	Tuesday	Wednesday	Thursday	Friday
8.45–9.10	← Registration P.H.S.E/independence, positioning →				
9.10–10.00	English	Literacy	Art	Science Half class horse riding alternate weeks	S English
10.00–10.30	Numeracy	English	→	→	Swimming
10.30–11.00	← P.H.S.E/independence/drinks/position →				
11.10–11.45	Literacy Lower school assembly	Humanities (history)	Maths/numeracy	Literacy	Humanities (geography)
11.45–1.00	← P.H.S.E (lunch preparation, feeding programmes/independence/positioning) →				
1.00–1.45	Music	Maths/numeracy	Literacy	Numeracy	Literacy
1.45–2.00	← Toileting programmes and repositioning →				
1.45–2.30	Half group P.H.S.E. (dressing) | Half group I.C.T	I.C.T.	CDT (design)	Half group I.C.T. sensory room | Half group P.E.	Music | Half group I.C.T. | Half group Sensory room
2.30–3.00	←	P.E./programme	→	→	
3.00–3.15	P.H.S.E./drinks	P.H.S.E./drinks	P.H.S.E./drinks	P.H.S.E/drinks	P.H.S.E/drinks
3.15–3.30	historical reflection spiritual reflection	historical reflection spiritual reflection	historical reflection spiritual reflection	historical reflection spiritual reflection	School Assembly

Modern Foreign Culture – Thailand Week beginning 9th October See individual timetables for therapy programmes Class topic – Light and Colour

Figure 7.1 *timetable*

Nursery Class 2000–2001

Class P	9:00–9:15	9:15–9:50	9:50–10:25	10:40–11:20	11:20–12:00	1:05–1:35	1:35–2:10	2:10–2:40	2:40–3:10
Monday	Reg.	English S and L News Pencil Skills	Swim	PHYSICAL Swimming (PE)		Knowledge and understanding (Science)		English Language Groups SALT	
Tuesday	Reg. Ass.	Maths/Numeracy Shape Size Colour	Maths/Numeracy Shape Size Colour	Literacy Story SALT	Literacy Pencil Skills	Creative (Art)		Technology DT	ICT
Wednesday	Reg.	Maths/ Numeracy Number Songs	RDA	PHYSICAL Horse Riding (PE)		English/ Communication		Creative (Music)	
Thursday	Reg. Ass.	English Language Groups	English Language Groups	Maths/Numeracy IEPs Messy Maths (Pre-Maths)	Maths/Numeracy IEPs Messy Maths (Pre-Maths)	Knowledge and understanding (Human & Social) PHYSIO		PSHE/ RE	
Friday	Reg. Ass.	Literacy Phonics ABC ORT Rhyme Time R-P2	Literacy Interactive Rhymes/ stories R-P2	Maths/Numeracy Games	R-P2	Structured Play Sensory Science			Creative (Singing)

The letters P L U S H E N C H appear vertically between columns spelling out groupings.

PSHE – Drinks time: developing drinking & eating skills, turn taking, interacting with peers, sharing, communicating (PECs) choice making, carrying out routine tasks.

Figure 7.2 *timetable*

Chapter 2). Timetabled inclusion opportunities within special schools can promote both social inclusion and access to the curriculum.

Within a class timetable there is a need to provide for a range of different pupil groupings, each of which has its advantages. All pupils, including those who experience PMLD, require some experience of specialist learning environments and interest-specific groupings. All pupils, again including those who experience PMLD, will also benefit from wide-ranging learning encounters shared with their age peers. This range of possibilities suggests a need for whole-school agreement on providing appropriate balance in the timetable.

Suggested groupings

Figure 7.3 reflects the possible groupings that pupils who experience PMLD may have access to at some point during their school day. This should be detailed on their individual timetables, and will influence the time allocation balance.

Group composition	Group characteristics	Lesson focus
Key Stage or age specific groups (inclusive group)	Pupils with varying past achievements, needs and experiences	Curriculum focused activities and experiences Tutor group sessions
Groups of pupils with similar abilities	Pupils of similar prior achievement Mix of year groups/Key Stages	Literacy Numeracy
Specialist needs	Pupils of similar needs for specialist approaches	Sensory, physical and personal approaches
Individual	Any pupil	One to one teaching, pastoral work, tutorial, guidance, therapies
Whole school	All pupils	Assembly, celebrating achievement, PSHE

Figure 7.3 *Possible groupings during a school day*

Where groupings are to be diverse, we suggest that:

- staff, for example subject-specialist teachers and class tutors, should collaborate over short term planning for pupils and students who experience PMLD ;
- when developing strategies for differentiating schemes of work, collaborative planning should focus on promoting meaningful participation, involvement and inclusion to the most appropriate extent rather than on separate activities;
- relevant priority targets from IEPs should 'move' with learners so that they are known and can be addressed by the staff working with that pupil in all contexts: thus pupils may carry 'passports' with them which detail prioritised targets from their IEP.

In this inclusive setting, two pupils share music together

Funding will be required to establish and support inclusive initiatives. For example, support staff should be placed with pupils where the need is greatest, depending both on the characteristics of each individual learner and on the degree of challenge to be met within inclusive activities. Staff will need time for joint planning and preparatory work. Trial projects and new initiatives, starting, for example, with the younger pupils, may demand additional levels of support on a temporary basis.

Chapter 8

Target setting

The next of the key structures which enable staff to construct a whole curriculum for pupils who experience PMLD is target setting. Special schools have in the past been accustomed to setting targets for individual pupils. However, target setting has gone further and, as a school improvement strategy, is now statutory as outlined in DfEE Circular 11/98 (1998c) and the revised version of Supporting the Target Setting Process (DfEE/QCA March 2001). Target setting is about having challenging yet realistic improvement goals for individual pupils, individual staff members and for the whole school.

The guideline to ensure that targets are worthwhile is that they are SMART:

Specific
Measurable
Achievable
Realistic
Time-specific

Targets for individual pupils are set in their IEPs. The revised SEN Code of Practice (DfES November 2001) suggests three to four key targets (4.27, p. 37) within IEPs that have been discussed with parents. These targets will reflect individual pupil priorities and may address key skills, the core curriculum of Mathematics, English, ICT and PSHE, and may be a behavioural or physical target depending on the pupil's special needs. The most effective pupil targets are those produced through collaborative professional planning, with individual pupil involvement where appropriate. A pupil's IEP targets should be made accessible to all members of his or her trans-disciplinary support network, and, where appropriate, made accessible to the pupil concerned by displaying them in the learning environment with photos and symbols, as needed. This will help to focus whole team work on helping pupils to achieve their set targets. It is important that the targets set are SMART enough to be achieved within a set timescale. The majority of targets will be quantitative, however, owing to the nature of some pupils who experience PMLD other targets will be more suited to qualitative assessment on an experiential level. Successful target setting is dependent on effective and accurate assessment, and is often the key to future planning.

Opportunities for assessment

To establish validity and 'best fit' within the assessed area a more realistic reflection of the pupil's learning and development is established if one member of staff acts as the validator. All staff should have a working knowledge of the IEP targets and be ready to record responses and outcomes on an ongoing basis. It is not appropriate for pupils who experience PMLD to sit SATs tests at the end of each Key Stage. Some special schools have therefore decided to use QCA framework for assessment (QCA/DfEE 2001) to assess pupils at the end of each Key Stage in order to show pupil progression.

In the past some schools have had to set zero targets as there were no appropriate levels of assessment within the National Curriculum for pupils who experience PMLD. Now, with the recent publication of *Planning, Teaching and Assessing the Curriculum for Pupils with Learning Difficulties* (DfEE/QCA 2001) we can offer an alternative by setting meaningful targets related to the P-Scales. The exemplar schemes of work in this book (see Part 4) set out 'opportunities for assessment' which the Group originally devised to be non-generic across all P-Levels. Therefore intended learning outcomes could also be adapted for target setting, anticipating that any child at a given level may strive to attain the next level, or breadth within a level, during the timescale relative to their individual needs. The range of teaching ideas offered in the exemplars allows for age appropriate activities to meet very early developmental steps for older aged pupils and for these targets to be achieved within a meaningful context.

Targets should be identified which incorporate opportunities for progress and progression for pupils who experience PMLD. Benefits of this type of target setting in relationship to teaching and learning are that it reflects the 'SMART-ness' of individual targets and allows for 'value added' purpose – that education for pupils who experience PMLD is valued within the whole school community and shown by inclusion into whole school development. It also shows improvement for those pupils who are progressing in the smallest steps within a P-Level and indicates whether using a target in the next P-Level may or may not be appropriate.

School targets

It is often difficult to set targets for a cohort of pupils who experience PMLD since targets are normally individualised and/or pupil specific. However, it may sometimes be appropriate to identify small group IEPs, and to develop a profile of individual targets which may be incorporated into a school target. This may, for example, reflect pupil attainment in a whole school's developmental process. As an example, a school target might be that 75 per cent of all pupil IEP targets should be met that school year.

Whole school targets can also be set which improve the teaching and learning process for all pupils, including those who experience PMLD, and are based on improving their learning environments. For example, a school may decide that all pupils will have access to a computer in their classroom by a certain date.

School INSET activities, as part of this whole school target-setting process, should be carefully planned, monitored and evaluated, with all activities focused on achieving the present target.

Professional development

Professional development should be led by pupils' needs and should be regularly reviewed as the range of pupil's needs changes. The allocation of resources for training should be included in the School Improvement Plan and needs to be flexible enough to reflect these changes. Subject

Coordinators need to keep abreast of the latest developments in their particular area and their relevance to pupils who experience PMLD. The Subject Leader should also be prepared to advise on and support the adaptation of the National Curriculum to make it meaningful for such pupils.

As part of a whole team approach all members should have equal access to relevant training in order to promote understanding and knowledge of the wide range of disability and the effect this has on pupil learning style. Commonality of practice across the whole school raises the awareness and knowledge base of all staff towards pupils who have a diversity of specific needs. Training would need to reflect an inclusive society and staff should 'learn to give away their knowledge and skills ... engaging in consultancy, demystifying expertise, exercising skills systematically and generally working in an open collaborative way' (Hegarty 1988).

Performance management now replaces staff appraisal, with both qualitative and quantitative evidence being collected to support individually agreed staff targets.

Chapter 9

Individual education plans

This chapter discusses the important role of individual education plans in the construction of a whole curriculum for pupils who experience PMLD. The best IEPs are those which are active documents, which show ongoing record keeping and assessment of pupil progress and progression, and which ideally are updated regularly with views and comments of all staff concerned.

We emphasise the real value of the writing and development of IEPs as a process rather than a static end-product. The identification of response to individual need and the consequent writing and development of IEPs as a process should be in accordance with the principles and procedures laid out in the Code of Practice (DFE 1994) and developed (for example) by Ramjhun (1995). Such planning should entail consultation with other professionals in the trans-disciplinary team; with parents and carers; and with pupils themselves, whenever appropriate and not simply at the Annual Review meeting itself – i.e. this should be part of an ongoing process of planning and regular review.

Paperwork associated with IEPs should show targets and the records of progress and achievement in relation to those targets. It may also include notes about teaching methods; contexts for learning; individual timetable modifications; and strategies for the management of pupils' physical, sensory or behavioural needs. Such notes may be presented in separate sections within IEP documentation.

Other points to bear in mind are that:

- there may be long (across a Key Stage), medium (annual) and short term (see below) phases in the development of IEPs;
- the short term elements of IEPs should include working documents which are 'crisply written' (DfEE 1998a, p. 16), easy to use, accessible and capable of being flexible and responsive;
- many teachers set a small number (varying in our group between one and six) of measurable short term targets in relation to priorities identified within statements. This is in line with the suggestion that IEPs should focus 'on three or four short-term targets for the child' (DfEE 1998a, p. 16 and DfES November 2001, p. 37) – see our earlier reference to SMART targets;
- the priority targets which are identified may not be subject-related but focus on key skills, as is emphasised in the *Programme of Action* (DfEE 1998a, p. 16), which states that targets within IEPs are 'generally most helpful when they relate to key skills, such as communication, literacy, numeracy, behaviour and social skills'.
- 'small steps' analysis of the 'core curriculum' can inform the setting of targets within IEPs so that they are relevant and achievable;

- some targets can be experimental and/or experiential in order to see what new responses may be elicited;
- maintenance or 'plateau' targets can also be important for some pupils.

Short term targets

Short term targets may encompass:

- current targets that are being extended into a new time frame;
- alternative targets, addressing new priorities, selected from aims established at Annual Review;
- previously set targets which are re-introduced for the purposes of consolidation, maintenance, generalisation or further refinement and development.

The targets should be :

- designed for achievement over a short period, such as a half term, and should be subject to regular review;
- integrated into medium term planning in relation to the curriculum and generalised into a range of settings.

The IEP can be used as a means of individualising the group timetable and facilitating short term adjustments to time allocation agreements for particular pupils. It is suggested, therefore, that there should be a whole school format for IEP planning to aid continuity.

All record keeping relating to the targets should be focused on significant, new responses and should avoid lengthy and repetitive narrative. These records should be kept in relation to both targets set within IEPs and the assessment opportunities established within schemes of work for the curriculum.

Some examples of medium and short-term IEPs are shown in Appendix 2.

Chapter 10

Schemes of work

This chapter discusses the important planning processes for schemes of work. Strategic planning for time allocation in the whole curriculum will ensure breadth, balance and relevance in schemes of work for all pupils. The development of relevant and accessible schemes of work will originate:

- with curriculum documents, for example, programmes of study for the subjects of the National Curriculum;
- with each school's own curriculum documentation, for example, for personal and social education;
- with commercially produced materials, such as EQUALs.

These schemes of work will be moderated in development, review and revision by perceptions about the range of pupils' current and prospective needs.

Drawing upon these original sources and influences, schools may create brief policy statements and more extensive guidelines for teaching staff which might incorporate guidance on access for pupils who experience PMLD: for example, clarifying the role of sensory approaches.

The purpose of the schemes of work themselves is to set out those experiences which should be common to groups of pupils, usually in age-related cohorts. The intention is that schemes of work are subject to review and so should be general enough to be used several times with different cohorts of pupils moving through particular age bands, i.e. specific topics repeated within a rolling programme of study.

The process of developing schemes of work will involve long term planning, planning for progression, medium term planning and short term planning.

Long term planning makes it possible to generate a 'map' of the curriculum for each age group in order to show, in outline:

- relationships between curriculum documentation, subject aims and programmes of study;
- the balance between different subjects and aspects of the whole curriculum;
- the balance between continuing work and blocked units for each subject;
- a rolling programme or cycle of blocked units, modules, themes or topics, each with an assessment focus;
- the important links between subjects;
- curricular options or opportunities for staff and pupils to explore

Long term planning

47

flexibility within the curriculum, e.g. reference to time and content allocations ;

● progression from Key Stage to Key Stage.

Planning for progression

All staff can contribute to constructing curriculum plans which provide for an appropriate progression from Key Stage to Key Stage. This, in turn, will enable members of the trans-disciplinary team to design and implement learning opportunities which promote progress and achievement for individual pupils throughout the whole curriculum.

Ouvry and Saunders (1996, p. 216) acknowledge that progression for pupils who experience PMLD 'may not always equate with moving up a hierarchy of achievement, which describes an ever-increasing level of skill or knowledge'.

In addition to working towards the acquisition of new skills, Ouvry and Saunders go on to suggest that 'we are also looking to increase understanding of experiences, to provide breadth and enable the pupil to carry out existing skills in different circumstances'.

This planning for progression in the curriculum for pupils who experience PMLD will take account of a range of different issues which contribute towards preparation for lifelong learning. With acknowledgement to the QCA curriculum guidelines (QCA/DfEE 2001), framework for assessment and our subsequent adaptations (see Chapter 6), and the analysis of progression provided by Byers and Rose (1996, p. 40), these issues may include:

● skill development – so that pupils are encouraged to gain new skills and/or to maintain, refine, consolidate, transfer or generalise existing skills;

● entitlement to curricular content – so that pupils' access to new areas of experience, knowledge and understanding is extended;

● the provision of a range of contexts for learning – ensuring, for example, that activities, resources, environments and the attitudes of staff and peers are appropriate to pupils' ages, interests and prior achievements;

● offering an ever broader range of teaching approaches – including experiential, sensory, behavioural, holistic and problem-solving methods – in order to facilitate fluency for pupils in an ever increasing variety of learning styles;

● bringing into use a developing variety of forms of equipment – for example, in support of environmental control, independent mobility and access to ICT – in order to offer pupils the maximum amount of control over their lives;

● providing a widening range of learning opportunities within and outside the special school – for example, through integration with their age peers and appropriate inclusion into mainstream schools and further education; and in real-life situations in the community;

● functional application – so that learners are enabled, as far as possible, to move away from dependence upon adult support and classroom-based activity, towards independence and practical activity oriented towards community participation.

Medium term planning should build upon the long term plan by providing greater detail:

- for blocked units, modules, themes or topics showing:
  - their position in the long term plan;
  - references to curriculum documentation;
  - intended learning or well-differentiated objectives;
  - a set of key activities, possibly in a week by week sequence, with an indication of optional extension activities, such as visits, field trips or opportunities for review and reflection;
  - opportunities for well-differentiated recording and assessment;

- for continuing work, showing:
  - hierarchies of developmentally sequential skills and competencies;
  - the content of repeated sessions;
  - sequences of activity through regular sessions;
  - ongoing, daily work.

Medium term plans should provide a supportive, but not prescriptive, level of detail in order to reduce the need for complex short term planning. It is our intention ultimately to streamline documentation and, in so doing, avoid burdensome bureaucratic tasks and eliminate repetition. Medium term plans may also show how work may be differentiated for groupings of pupils or students at each age stage; for example, group education plans can be used for:

- bringing together shared objectives for pupils with similar ability;
- facilitating peer group activities from a 'buddying' perspective;
- managing resources, including classroom staff.

In order to promote the inclusion of pupils who experience PMLD, this will often mean providing a sensory dimension to such activities, through touching, feeling, listening, seeing or smelling (as discussed previously). In this way, sensory work becomes an approach to teaching and a mode through which learning may be facilitated rather than a separate curriculum area. It should therefore be an increasingly important element of medium term planning.

Medium term planning

Short term planning is specific to a class or group and may encompass:

- weekly planning formats;
- daily planning, for example, through teachers' files and diaries;
- lesson plans.

Because short term planning is ephemeral and subject to alteration in the light of unforeseen circumstances, it will be neither realistic nor efficient to expect experienced staff to formalise a lesson plan for each and every session of each and every day. Where medium term plans relating to the curriculum are secure and sufficiently detailed, and where IEPs show targets which constitute short term priorities specific to individual pupils, short term planning may remain relatively informal. Further, short term planning should be flexible enough to allow for some spontaneity in responding to pupil interests, local, national or global events, and unforeseen eventualities.

Short term planning

Experiencing rhythm in different ways

While there may be no requirement to generate formal paper plans for each and every lesson, the short term planning process is crucial. It enables staff to differentiate long and medium term plans for particular learners (for example, in order to promote access for an individual pupil who experiences PMLD through a specific sensory route); to integrate targets from pupils' IEPs into classroom activity with groups of pupils; and to share understandings about objectives, methods and outcomes with other adults in the classroom.

The process of short term planning may also be used by staff in order to:

- plan teaching methods, pupil groupings and organisational issues;
- provide notes about, and allocate responsibilities for, pupils' positioning, movement, mobility and comfort;
- deploy staff effectively and manage the use of resources and equipment;
- support detailed planning for new or unfamiliar sessions;
- build up a library of lesson plans as a useful point of reference for future planning.

Short term plans also link with timetables, staffing, rotas and individual plans for the care and management of pupils with complex physical or para-medical needs.

It may be useful for subject co-ordinators to work with colleagues, perhaps as a part of their subject monitoring role, in order to formalise successful short term plans as exemplars. These illustrative samples can then be collected together within schemes of work documentation in order to help staff to control repetition, to promote progression or to inspire new developments. However, short term plans are not intended to be used with different groups of pupils on a number of occasions.

Chapter 11

Record keeping, assessment, reporting and review

In this chapter and the previous one, we have assumed that schools will wish to negotiate a common core to whole school planning and record keeping systems which all members of staff will be expected to use. Beyond this common core, staff may be required to undertake further tasks with pupils in certain age groups – for example, Baseline Assessment in Early Years. They may also decide to undertake additional planning and record keeping, according to their own preferences.

It is important to maintain records of experience, response, progress and achievement which relate to targets in pupils' IEPs and which drive the interim reviews of targets and the Annual Review process as well as informing progress files. Such records should also relate to schemes of work for the curriculum and promote continuous assessment and annual reporting as well as informing progress files.

In particular a pupil's ongoing Record of Achievement should include:

- carefully annotated and dated samples of work;
- photographs, tape or video sequences;
- various forms of pupil self-assessment.

In practice, record keeping may take a number of forms, each suited to particular aspects of the record keeping agenda. It may be necessary to keep:

- extracts from schemes of work, in so far as they can be considered a record of experience;
- diary records of pupil responses;
- notes and records kept by teachers and other members of staff.

The records kept should be informative and purposeful while being as streamlined as possible and should avoid duplication or overlap of information.

As it is neither possible, nor appropriate, to maintain an exhaustive written log of everything that each pupil experiences and achieves, it is necessary to develop strategies for focusing the record keeping task. This can be achieved by, for example:

- devoting some time in each unit of work to review and reflect, allowing staff to concentrate on observation, recording and assessment;
- using one lesson each week, focusing on different aspects of the curriculum in turn, for observation, recording and assessment;

- targeting particular pupils for observation, recording and assessment in particular lessons, ensuring that all learners are assessed in all subjects over time;
- using short term planning structures to allocate responsibility for observation, recording and assessment to specified members of staff in specified lessons;
- focusing recording on 'significant, new responses' (SCAA 1996a).

Of course, record keeping procedures must also be flexible enough to allow for the noting of unlooked-for, spontaneous or unusual responses, whenever, wherever or with whomever these may occur. It follows that all members of the multi-disciplinary team should have access to records and should feel confident in making focused and relevant contributions. This requirement may have implications for policy and practice in professional collaboration, trans-disciplinary responsibilities and shared curriculum and professional development (Lacey and Lomas 1993).

Learners themselves will also benefit from opportunities to make records and assessments of their experiences and achievements to inform their Records of Achievement. For those pupils and students who experience PMLD, strategies for self-review, self-recording and self-assessment will need to be diverse, multi-modal and, often, idiosyncratic (Lawson 1998; SCAA 1996b).

Part 4
Practical materials

Chapter 12
Rationale

In this book, the Group has set out to offer practical help and advice for those professionals, parents and other members of the trans-disciplinary network who are working with pupils who experience PMLD in the QCA framework for assessment using the criteria for P-Levels 1 to 3(ii). The focus has ranged from the entitlement, enablement and empowerment of pupils who experience PMLD to equality of access to a wide range of enriched learning opportunities.

Choosing the three core areas from the National Curriculum (English, Maths and Science), we have developed selected strands into exemplar schemes of work which show learning objectives, experiences and ideas for curriculum with a means for meaningful assessment. Our experience and knowledge gained over many years of working with pupils who experience PMLD have been pooled to develop a basis which professionals, parents and other members of the trans-disciplinary network may adapt in order to respond to the needs of their pupils in both special and inclusive settings.

These exemplars should not be taken as conclusive, but as guidance for all staff to use as a springboard for their own ideas. The assessment phrase used: 'within an English/Maths/Science context' is not intended to be limiting, rather to emphasise that assessment of specific intended learning outcomes may be more effectively realised within focused learning environments. For example, if a pupil who experiences PMLD demonstrates an awareness – P-Level 1(ii) – of a specific stimulus within a session focused on Science, then this should be recorded as such. The same pupil may also demonstrate a similar awareness of maths-focused stimulus, such as counting games, and, again, this should be assessed as an intended learning outcome within Maths. The learning environment is the key: teachers in mainstream schools would not expect their pupils to gain new maths skills in an English lesson, or learn about Shakespeare in a Science lesson. (Enlightenment could happen, since learning is cross-curricular, but from an assessment point of view new maths skills are usually assessed within Maths lessons.) However, although a pupil who experiences PMLD is entitled to have his or her intended learning outcomes assessed within specific learning contexts, assessment opportunities are more likely to be ongoing and relative to a pupil's IEP.

In order to enable maximum pupil progress and participation we have allowed for pupils' individual learning targets, embedded in curriculum planning, to be developed. Progress for some of our pupils will be very slow and a pupil who experiences PMLD may be working within a particular P-Level for some, or all, of their time. In order to offer a rich, challenging curriculum a range of experiences are recommended within each level.

In terms of assessment, the levels of descriptions outlined are intended to assist in making summative judgements about pupils' experiences and achievements, which in turn inform target setting and reporting.

At Key Stage 4 the curriculum for pupils who experience PMLD often diversifies from the National Curriculum and follows the ALL, ASDAN or individual school programmes of study rather than the (for them) more abstract National Curriculum Key Stage 4 programmes.

It is possible to offer schemes of work which complement the child's interests and to continue with a strand from an earlier Key Stage. At Key Stage 4 our pupils may be best served by being offered a more diverse and/or deeper access to these previous Key Stages, or by covering subjects of the National Curriculum through other accredited curricula. As there is a legal entitlement to the freedom to teach from a previous Key Stage this should not cause a problem.

We hope that this book proves helpful in setting effective individual pupil targets as part of a larger curriculum plan that enables the measurement of pupil progress up to P-Level 4 of the National Curriculum and as a possible basis for monitoring school improvement.

Chapter 13
Exemplar schemes of work

One of the most challenging aspects of working with pupils who experience PMLD is to find a means of facilitating progress along often highly individual pathways to learning that not only are age appropriate but also convey specific learning objectives. We have offered activities which fall within this brief. As we have approached each Key Stage we have endeavoured to present a format that allows learners to become enabled as far as possible towards greater autonomy, to address the barriers to their learning and move away from a culture of dependence on adult support. We have also suggested ways in which class based activities could move more towards those which support planned independence and interdependence oriented towards greater participation in the community.

The schemes of work are arranged as follows:

English

English Key Stage 1
Attainment Target 1: Speaking & Listening
Key Concept: Pupils should work towards communicating confidently with different people

P-Level	Intended Learning Outcomes	Experiences and Activities	Assessment Opportunities
1(i)	**Encounter** ● a range of multi-sensory stimuli within an English setting	*Facilitation through an environment which includes…* ● adult/peer describing the journey/environment as pupils encounter their home or school surroundings ● people talking through daily routines with pupils using photos and objects of reference ● joining peer groups to encounter drama work, share lunchtimes, free time etc. ● being helped to press 'Big Mac' switch to say a greeting or farewell ● hearing a range of familiar voices talking, singing and reading both as part of open class ethos and at a personal one to one level (e.g. for Intensive Interaction) ● sharing regular small group work where pupils encounter reference to their names, e.g. restriction, where personal items can be used to develop sense of self	*Within an English context pupil is present and passive, participation is fully prompted,* and will make… ● random involuntary movements, e.g. eye flicker, change in body tone
1(ii)	**Awareness of** ● a range of multi-sensory stimuli within an English setting	*Facilitation through an environment which includes the above, plus…* ● playing peek-a-boo games with a variety of adults and children ● being aware of touch and being touched by people when pupils are spoken to ● sharing regular circle times with classmates and peer groups ● using echo mike to enhance and enjoy vocalising ● other members of the class communicating with both pupils and adults ● recorded 'conversations' played back to evoke responses and awareness of own voice ● sharing use of a 'Big Mac' switch to greet friends, peers and familiar adults ● sharing extended contact with one communicating person in activities such as message, physiotherapy, hydrotherapy, aromatherapy	*Within an English context pupil shows reflex and intermittent reactions, emerging awareness, inconsistent and affective responses by…* ● tolerating a range of sensory stimulation: i) tactile ii) auditory iii) visual iv) gustatory v) olfactory vi) kinaesthetic

English Key Stage: 1
Attainment Target 1: Speaking & Listening
Key Concept: Pupils should work towards communicating confidently with different people

P-Level	Intended Learning Outcomes	Experiences and Activities	Assessment Opportunities

2(i)	**Respond/React**
	• to a range of multi-sensory stimuli within an English setting
		Facilitation through an environment which includes the above plus…
		• use of echo mike to promote 'conversations'
		• looking in mirror
		• pulling faces with both adults and friends to exaggerate emotions
		• developing personal method for displaying likes and dislikes (body language, vocalisations and facial expression)
		• use of objects of reference to cue pupil in to activity
		• offering and responding to choices for self-expression
		• listening to recordings of environmental sounds that are associated with tasks and activities
			Within an English context pupil shows interest and reactive responses, focussed attention and co-actively explores and investigates by…
			• responding to immediate sensory stimulation
			• responding to adult interactions
			• responding when stimulus stops
			• responding to remote sensory stimulation by…
			  i) voluntary movement e.g. change in facial expression, arm or leg movement
			  ii) eye tracking
			  iii) ear tracking (turns head)
			  iv) vocalising

2(ii)	**Pro-active Co-operation** • within a range of multi-sensory activities and objects within an English setting	*Facilitation through an environment which includes the above, plus…* • use of Intensive Interaction to promote conversations • use of mirrors in drama work and paired work to develop sense of self • developing and continuing choice-making activities through the use of objects of reference and photographs • use of visual and tactile timetables to facilitate pupils' awareness of daily routines • hearing different voice tones: loud/soft and with regional accents	*Within an English context pupil remembers learned responses and is pro-active by…* • glancing alternately at two stimuli • reacting consistently to the same stimuli • expressing likes and dislikes consistently • retaining object momentarily without casting • making general exploratory movements

English Key Stage: 1
Attainment Target 1: Speaking & Listening
Key Concept: Pupils should work towards communicating confidently with different people

P-Level	Intended Learning Outcomes	Experiences and Activities	Assessment Opportunities

3(i)	**Intentionally Participate**
	
	• with a range of multi-sensory stimuli within an English setting
		Facilitation through an environment which includes the above plus…
		
		• use of communication aids to greet family and friends
		• use of communication aids take messages home to parents and carers
		• pick up a symbol, photo to obtain a desired object or activity independently
		• listen to plays, stories and poems read aloud or from tapes, CDs, and the computer such as ORT resources, Sherston Naughty Stories, Fuzzbuzz etc. and stories and songs on the Internet
		• use of photos, symbols or signs for choice-making in real situations outside of school
		
		(ORT = Oxford Reading Tree)
			Within an English context pupil demonstrates an ability to…
			
			• sustain concentration
			• display interested observation, e.g.
			  i) focused looking
			  ii) listening
			  iii) reaching
			
			• make pre verbal communication responses, e.g.
			  i) pointing to objects or events
			  ii) searching for an object after it has 'disappeared'
			  iii) searching for a stimulus after it has stopped
			  iv) choosing to participate (or not)
			  v) seeking attention
			
			• explore in a more diverse way, e.g.
			  i) rubs
			  ii) bangs
			  iii) pushes
			  iv) pulls
			  v) squeezes
			  vi) presses

English Key Stage: 1
Attainment Target 1: Speaking & Listening
Key Concept: Pupils should work towards communicating confidently with different people

P-Level	Intended Learning Outcomes	Experiences and Activities	Assessment Opportunities

3(ii)	**Initiate**
	
	 • within a range of multi-sensory stimuli in an English setting
		Facilitation through an environment which includes the above, plus….
		
		 • engaging adult interactions using smiles, eye contact and/or vocalisations
		 • participating in class or school assemblies, shows and reviews
		 • using communication aids to greet familiar people independently
		 • picking up a symbol or make a sign to choose a song or activity from a range of choices
		 • using photos, objects of reference or symbols to develop skills in using a personalised timetable and being expected to link timetable to specific events during the day
			Within an English context pupil demonstrates an ability to…
			
			 • anticipate known events, follow routines
			 • initiate interactions, activities
			 • actively explore objects/events for more extended periods
			 • take turns in shared activities
			 • use emerging conventional communication by…
			   i) greeting familiar people
			   ii) attempting to sign
			   iii) using symbols
			   iv) recognising photographs
			   v) using objects of reference

English Key Stage: 1
Attainment Target 2: Reading
Key Concept: Pupils should develop visual and auditory awareness through sharing interactive literacy resources

P-Level	Intended Learning Outcomes	Experiences and Activities	Assessment Opportunities
1(i)	**Encounter** • a range of multi-sensory stimuli within an English setting	*Facilitation through an environment which includes…* • tactile manipulation of a variety of books • sharing a variety of age-appropriate texts • being part of a group experiencing poems and songs • exploring objects related to characters and events within the story • adult to describe events to child • being supported to hold and explore tactile/fluorescent letters • hearing familiar voices reading texts	*Within an English context pupil is present and passive, participation is fully prompted,* *and will make…* • random involuntary movements, e.g. eye flicker, change in body tone

1(ii)	**Awareness of**
	
	• a range of multi-sensory stimuli within an English setting
		Facilitation through an environment which includes the above, plus…
		
		• feeling and turning pages of a book
		• using tactile books for exploration
		• looking at the front cover, pictures and print
		• using props to support story, poem, song
		• using sensory cues to link with the text
		• adult signing letters on hand related to the tactile or visual letters
		• use of switches to access stories, e.g. 'Big Mac' switch with repeated phrase of story recorded
			Within an English context pupil shows reflex and intermittent reactions, emerging awareness, inconsistent and affective responses by…
			
			• tolerating a range of sensory stimulation:
			
			  i) tactile
			  ii) auditory
			  iii) visual
			  iv) gustatory
			  v) olfactory
			  vi) kinaesthetic

English Key Stage: 1
Attainment Target 2: Reading
Key Concept: Pupils should develop visual and auditory awareness through sharing interactive literacy resources

P-Level	Intended Learning Outcomes	Experiences and Activities	Assessment Opportunities

2(i)	**Respond/React**
	
	 • to a range of multi-sensory stimuli within an English setting
		Facilitation through an environment which includes the above, plus…
		
		 • use of props when telling stories to add dimension to the content
		 • helping to turn pages
		 • touching and/or looking at the pictures or objects related to the text
		 • use of a tactile-story sack
		 • use of and reference to auditory and visual cues within a text
		 • developing visual attention to the adult telling or reading the text
		 • being given auditory/visual/tactile and olfactory cues for songs, poems and rhymes
		 • adults to sign the key words in a story to pupils and link to props
		 • sharing individualised photo albums
			Within an English context pupil shows interest and reactive responses, focused attention and co-actively explores and investigates by…
			
			 • responding to immediate sensory stimulation
			 • responding to adult interactions
			 • responding when stimulus stops
			 • responding to remote sensory stimulation by…
			   i) voluntary movement, e.g. change in facial expression, arm or leg movement
			   ii) eye tracking
			   iii) ear tracking (turns head)
			   iv) vocalising

2(ii)	**Pro-active Co-operation** • within a range of multi-sensory activities and objects within an English setting	*Facilitation through an environment which includes the above, plus…* • use of switches to turn pages of a story on a computer • sharing group story sessions using switches, attempting gestures or signs • working alongside peers to listen to stories • selecting stories by using objects of reference or associated photo • experiencing a wide range of literary texts facilitated through photos, symbols, pictures and other visual stimuli • access to song, rhyme and story tapes with associated pictures/imagery • use of photo or symbol for a key word e.g. want/like • use of mirrors to develop sense of self, matching to photos of self	*Within an English context pupil remembers learned responses and is pro-active by…* • glancing alternately at two stimuli • reacting consistently to the same stimuli • expressing likes and dislikes consistently • retaining object momentarily without casting • making general exploratory movements

English Key Stage: 1
Attainment Target 2: Reading
Key Concept: Pupils should develop visual and auditory awareness through sharing interactive literacy resources

P-Level	Intended Learning Outcomes	Experiences and Activities	Assessment Opportunities

3(i)	**Intentionally Participate**
	
	● with a range of multi-sensory stimuli within an English setting
		Facilitation through an environment which includes the above, plus…
		
		● turn taking within story time
		● taking part in drama sessions associated with story
		● holding artefacts associated with story at appropriate moment
		● making choices of story or song using photo, symbol or object of reference
		● use of 'Big Mac 'to participate in repeated phrases of text
		● use of photograph, symbol or sign/gesture to participate in the story telling
		● establishing use of PECS programme where pupils are encouraged to identify visual cues (photo/picture/symbol) of preferred motivators
			Within an English context pupil demonstrates an ability to…
			
			● sustain concentration
			● display interested observation, e.g.
			  i) focused looking
			  ii) listening
			  iii) reaching
			
			● make pre verbal communication responses, e.g.
			  i) pointing to objects or events
			  ii) searching for an object after it has 'disappeared'
			  iii) searching for a stimulus after it has stopped
			  iv) choosing to participate (or not)
			  v) seeking attention
			
			● explore in a more diverse way, e.g.
			  i) rubs
			  ii) bangs
			  iii) pushes
			  iv) pulls
			  v) squeezes
			  vi) presses

English Key Stage: 1
Attainment Target 2: Reading
Key Concept: Pupils should develop visual and auditory awareness through sharing interactive literacy resources

P-Level	Intended Learning Outcomes	Experiences and Activities	Assessment Opportunities
3(ii)	**Initiate** • within a range of multi-sensory stimuli in an English setting	*Facilitation through an environment which includes the above, plus…* • initiating/responding to/continuing adult interactions • use of picture sequences to tell story, be it photo, symbol or object of reference • recognising and using artefacts from within story, poem and song • listening to different people read stories • having a reading partner from their peer group whom they join to share texts on a regular basis • permanent easy access to photographs of familiar objects and people (for use when initiating interaction/communicating choices) • a range of photos/symbols for matching to familiar objects/people/places • developing use of PECS programmes where pupils are encouraged to identify visual cues and use to initiate responses from staff/peers/family	*Within an English context pupil demonstrates an ability to…* • anticipate known events, follow routines • initiate interactions, activities • actively explore objects/events for more extended periods • take turns in shared activities • use emerging conventional communication by… 　i) greeting familiar people 　ii) attempting to sign 　iii) using symbols 　iv) recognising photographs 　v) using objects of reference

English Key Stage: 1
Attainment Target 3: Writing
Key Concept: Pupils should work towards developing fine motor perception skills

P-Level	Intended Learning Outcomes	Experiences and Activities	Assessment Opportunities
1(i)	**Encounter** • a range of multi-sensory stimuli within an English setting	*Facilitation through an environment which includes…* • assistance in manipulating dough • feeling rough or silky materials • having hands placed in soapy water • surrounding hands in dry and wet pasta • adult to describe the textures to pupil, eg when exploring objects hidden in sand • being helped to handle toys and tactile materials	*Within an English context pupil is present and passive, participation is fully prompted,* and will make… • random involuntary movements, e.g. eye flicker, change in body tone
1(ii)	**Awareness of** • a range of multi-sensory stimuli within an English setting	*Facilitation through an environment which includes the above, plus…* • making textured mobiles • sensory stimulation using objects/stimuli relating to themselves, e.g. 'Big Mac' with familiar recorded sound • visual representations of numerals • use of switches to access stories, e.g. 'Big Mac' switch with repeated phrase of story recorded • being helped to handle different media and the activity described to the pupil • exploring sensory paint: bright colours, associated sounds/smells	*Within an English context pupil shows reflex and intermittent reactions, emerging awareness, inconsistent and affective responses by…* • tolerating a range of sensory stimulation: i) tactile ii) auditory iii) visual iv) gustatory v) olfactory vi) kinaesthetic

English Key Stage: 1
Attainment Target 3: Writing
Key Concept: Pupils should work towards developing fine motor perception skills

P-Level	Intended Learning Outcomes	Experiences and Activities	Assessment Opportunities

2(i)	**Respond/React**
	• to a range of multi-sensory stimuli within an English setting
		Facilitation through an environment which includes the above, plus…
		• using computer programmes such as 'Draw' to encourage pupils to make their own 'stories'
		• use of props when telling stories to add dimension to the content
		• handling different media to develop tactile sensation and tolerance
		• having co-active support for hand stretching, reaching, grasping and moving objects or toys
		• being helped to look at or hold a photo, object of reference which is exchanged for the real thing
			Within an English context pupil shows interest and reactive responses, focused attention and co-actively explores and investigates by…
			• responding to immediate sensory stimulation
			• responding to adult interactions
			• responding when stimulus stops
			• responding to remote sensory stimulation by…
			  i) voluntary movement, e.g. change in facial expression, arm or leg movement
			  ii) eye tracking
			  iii) ear tracking (turns head)
			  iv) vocalising

2(ii)	**Pro-active Co-operation** • within a range of multi-sensory activities and objects within an English setting	*Facilitation through an environment which includes the above, plus…* • opportunities to use switches to develop cause and effect, and making choices, e.g. between two tastes offered, or activities in the sensory room • blowing balloons up to develop anticipation • playing 'boo!' using various fabrics • being encouraged to use a palmar grip to hold object and toys • being supported to make marks in different media	*Within an English context pupil remembers learned responses and is pro-active by…* • glancing alternately at two stimuli • reacting consistently to the same stimuli • expressing likes and dislikes consistently • retaining object momentarily without casting • making general exploratory movements

English Key Stage: 1
Attainment Target 3: Writing
Key Concept: Pupils should work towards developing fine motor perception skills

P-Level	Intended Learning Outcomes	Experiences and Activities	Assessment Opportunities

3(i)	**Intentionally Participate**
	
	• with a range of multi-sensory stimuli within an English setting
		Facilitation through an environment which includes the above, plus…
		
		• turn taking within story time
		• making marks on paper using paints, felt tips etc.
		• making hand or foot print paintings
		• use of wet sand to make hand impressions
		• making face paint pictures
		• reaching for and manipulating objects related to stories in literacy
			Within an English context pupil demonstrates an ability to…
			
			• sustain concentration
			• display interested observation, e.g.
			  i) focused looking
			  ii) listening
			  iii) reaching
			
			• make pre verbal communication responses, e.g.
			  i) pointing to objects or events
			  ii) searching for an object after it has 'disappeared'
			  iii) searching for a stimulus after it has stopped
			  iv) choosing to participate (or not)
			  v) seeking attention
			
			• explore in a more diverse way, e.g.
			  i) rubs
			  ii) bangs
			  iii) pushes
			  iv) pulls
			  v) squeezes
			  vi) presses

English Key Stage: 1
Attainment Target 3: Writing
Key Concept: Pupils should work towards developing fine motor perception skills

P-Level	Intended Learning Outcomes	Experiences and Activities	Assessment Opportunities

3(ii)	**Initiate**
	
	 • within a range of multi-sensory stimuli in an English setting
		Facilitation through an environment which includes the above, plus…
		
		 • using fingers to make marks in sand
		 • posting items into boxes
		 • stacking rings onto poles
		 • use 'Touch Screen' on computer for cause and effect work
		 • manipulating and selecting preferred items from boxes/bags etc.
		 • extending fingers to feel objects
		 • making marks independently with crayons and looking at marks made
		 • reaching out and holding an object at the right time in the story
			Within an English context pupil demonstrates an ability to…
			
			 • anticipate known events, follow routines
			 • initiate interactions, activities
			 • actively explore objects/events for more extended periods
			 • take turns in shared activities
			 • use emerging conventional communication by…
			   i) greeting familiar people
			   ii) attempting to sign
			   iii) using symbols
			   iv) recognising photographs
			   v) using objects of reference

English Key Stage: 2
Attainment Target 1: Speaking & Listening
Key Concept: Pupils should work towards communicating confidently with different people

P-Level	Intended Learning Outcomes	Experiences and Activities	Assessment Opportunities
1(i)	**Encounter** • a range of multi-sensory stimuli within an English setting	*Facilitation through an environment which includes…* • adult / peer talking about / referring to something specific associated with the environment as pupils encounter their home or school surroundings • familiar people talking through daily routines using photos and objects of reference • joining peer groups to encounter drama work, share lunchtimes, free time etc. to hear conversations • meeting familiar people in different settings • hearing a range of familiar voices talking, singing and reading both as part of open class ethos and at a personal one to one level (e.g. for intensive interaction) • sharing regular small group work where pupils encounter reference to their names, e.g. registration, where personal items can be used to develop sense of self • listening to taped stories (age appropriate)	*Within an English context pupil is present and passive, participation is fully prompted,* *and will make…* • random involuntary movements, e.g. eye flicker, change in body tone

1(ii)	**Awareness of**
	
	• a range of multi-sensory stimuli within an English setting
		Facilitation through an environment which includes the above, plus…
		
		• being talked through and prepared for both routine and occasional activities with enough space and time to adjust to new activity
		• being aware of touch and being touched by people when pupils are spoken to
		• participating in regular group times (including circle time) with peer groups
		• use of echo mike to promote vocalising and turn taking
		• recorded 'conversations' played back to evoke responses and develop awareness of own voice
		• meeting and greeting class visitors and familiar people in different settings
		• staff / family / peers making eye contact with the pupil and use of visual materials to enhance communication
		• having a range of objects to hold associated with familiar people
			Within an English context pupil shows reflex and intermittent reactions, emerging awareness, inconsistent and affective responses by…
			
			• tolerating a range of sensory stimulation:
			
			  i) tactile
			  ii) auditory
			  iii) visual
			  iv) gustatory
			  v) olfactory
			  vi) kinaesthetic

English Key Stage: 2
Attainment Target 1: Speaking & Listening
Key Concept: Pupils should work towards communicating confidently with different people

P-Level	Intended Learning Outcomes	Experiences and Activities	Assessment Opportunities

2(i)	**Respond/React**
	• to a range of multi-sensory stimuli within an English setting
		Facilitation through an environment which includes the above, plus…
		• use of gestures, facial expressions and sounds for greeting in different community settings
		• use of photos to encourage choices for self expression
		• being encouraged to show preferences
		• being part of turn taking activities with members of the class and people outside, through games and ICT skills
		• use of individualised ICT to greet people around the school and enjoy responses from familiar people having being helped to use switch which activates a hello message, e.g. on 'Big Mac' switch
		• looking at or eye pointing to a photo or symbol
		• recorded 'partner conversations' played back to evoke responses and develop awareness of own voice and that of familiar partner, e.g. Mum or Dad
			Within an English context pupil shows interest and reactive responses, focused attention and co-actively explores and investigates by…
			• responding to immediate sensory stimulation
			• responding to adult interactions
			• responding when stimulus stops
			• responding to remote sensory stimulation by…
			  i) voluntary movement, e.g. change in facial expression, arm or leg movement
			  ii) eye tracking
			  iii) ear tracking (turns head)
			  iv) vocalising

2(ii)	**Pro-active Co-operation** • within a range of multi-sensory activities and objects within an English setting	*Facilitation through an environment which includes the above, plus…* • use of switches to promote communication with staff, family and peers, e.g. pupil could be helped to take messages to different people and classes • developing and continuing choice-making activities through the use of objects of reference and symbols • use of a tactile and sensory timetable to facilitate pupils' awareness of daily routines • taking part in activities around the school with other pupils and adults • developing use of a photo or symbol to express feelings to familiar adults, e.g. like/dislike, happy/sad	*Within an English context pupil remembers learned responses and is pro-active by…* • glancing alternately at two stimuli • reacting consistently to the same stimuli • expressing likes and dislikes consistently • retaining object momentarily without casting • making general exploratory movements

English Key Stage: 2
Attainment Target 1: Speaking & Listening
Key Concept: Pupils should work towards communicating confidently with different people

P-Level	Intended Learning Outcomes	Experiences and Activities	Assessment Opportunities

3(i)	**Intentionally Participate**
	
	● with a range of multi-sensory stimuli within an English setting
		Facilitation through an environment which includes the above, plus…
		
		● use of communication aids with a variety of familiar people for different purposes
		● use of communication aids to take messages home to parents and friends and share messages brought back to class from home/friends
		● opportunities to seek and maintain attention
		● use of symbols, photos to obtain a desired object independently
		● listen to age appropriate plays, stories and poems read aloud or from tapes, CDs, and the computer
		● visiting cafés and other public places and asking for items using communication aids
		● valued inclusion in peer group and whole school assemblies
			Within an English context pupil demonstrates an ability to…
			
			● sustain concentration
			● display interested observation, e.g.
			  i) focused looking
			  ii) listening
			  iii) reaching
			
			● make pre verbal communication responses, e.g.
			  i) pointing to objects or events
			  ii) searching for an object after it has 'disappeared'
			  iii) searching for a stimulus after it has stopped
			  iv) choosing to participate (or not)
			  v) seeking attention
			
			● explore in a more diverse way, e.g.
			  i) rubs
			  ii) bangs
			  iii) pushes
			  iv) pulls
			  v) squeezes
			  vi) presses

English Key Stage: 2
Attainment Target 1: Speaking & Listening
Key Concept: Pupils should work towards communicating confidently with different people

P-Level	Intended Learning Outcomes	Experiences and Activities	Assessment Opportunities
3(ii)	**Initiate** • within a range of multi-sensory stimuli in an English setting	*Facilitation through an environment which includes the above, plus…* • initiating/respond to/continue adult interactions • use of picture sequences to tell story, be it photo, symbol or object of reference • recognising and using artefacts from within story, poem and song • listening to different people read stories • have a reading partner from their peer group whom they join and share texts on a regular basis • visiting library and/or book shop and choose books, (could work with reading partner) • matching photos or symbol or picture or object related to the text • use of switches to participate in the right place in the story • developing use of PECS programmes where pupils are encouraged to identify and share visual cues of preferred motivators, and use to initiate responses from peers/staff/family • permanent easy access to photographs of familiar objects and people (for use when initiating interaction/communicating choices)	*Within an English context pupil demonstrates an ability to…* • anticipate known events, follow routines • initiate interactions, activities • actively explore objects/events for more extended periods • take turns in shared activities • use emerging conventional communication by… i) greeting familiar people ii) attempting to sign iii) using symbols iv) recognising photographs v) using objects of reference

English Key Stage: 2
Attainment Target 2: Reading
Key Concept: Pupil should develop visual and auditory awareness through sharing interactive literacy resources

P-Level	Intended Learning Outcomes	Experiences and Activities	Assessment Opportunities
1(i)	**Encounter** ● a range of multi-sensory stimuli within an English setting	*Facilitation through an environment which includes…* ● tactile manipulation of a variety of books, magazines, letters ● opportunities to share and experience a range of different stories, rhymes and songs with staff, families, peers ● exploring articles related to events within the story ● being part of a peer group experiencing a variety of age appropriate texts ● using photographs or objects related to the text ● being supported to hold/share tactile letters with sensory elements ● sharing different text genres, e.g. spooky story!	*Within an English context pupil is present and passive, participation is fully prompted,* and will make… ● random involuntary movements, e.g. eye flicker, change in body tone
1(ii)	**Awareness of** ● a range of multi-sensory stimuli within an English setting	*Facilitation through an environment which includes the above, plus…* ● feeling and turning pages of books/magazine ● encouraging pupils to develop visual attention skills to the reader and objects or photos used for enhancing texts ● supported use of switches to access stories, e.g. 'Big Mac' switch with repeated phrase of story recorded	*Within an English context pupil shows reflex and intermittent reactions, emerging awareness, inconsistent and affective responses by…* ● tolerating a range of sensory stimulation: i) tactile ii) auditory iii) visual iv) gustatory v) olfactory vi) kinaesthetic

English Key Stage: 2
Attainment Target 2: Reading
Key Concept: Pupil should develop visual and auditory awareness through sharing interactive literacy resources

P-Level	Intended Learning Outcomes	Experiences and Activities	Assessment Opportunities
2(i)	**Respond/React** ● to a range of multi-sensory stimuli within an English setting	*Facilitation through an environment which includes the above, plus…* ● use of props when telling stories to add dimension to the content ● use of a tactile-story sack ● use of and reference to sensory cues to enhance the experience of the text, including buzzers, smells, sound tapes etc. ● seeing key words in the story reading being signed ● being helped to focus on pictures through good positioning of book and lighting ● exploring tactile letters: wooden, sandpaper, foam, plastic ● continuing to develop visual attention to story reader/teller ● sharing individualised photo albums	*Within an English context pupil shows interest and reactive responses, focused attention and co-actively explores and investigates by…* ● responding to immediate sensory stimulation ● responding to adult interactions ● responding when stimulus stops ● responding to remote sensory stimulation by… i) voluntary movement, e.g. change in facial expression, arm or leg movement ii) eye tracking iii) ear tracking (turns head) iv) vocalising
2(ii)	**Pro-active Co-operation** ● within a range of multi-sensory activities and objects within an English setting	*Facilitation through an environment which includes the above, plus…* ● use of switches to turn pages of a story on a computer ● participating within group story sessions ● working alongside peers to listen to stories ● reading to pupils and waiting for a responsive gesture or vocalisation ● encouraging signing attempts, e.g. through use of co-active signing ● opportunities for longer eye contact and visual fixation of real objects or photos ● linking objects to pictures in books/magazines etc ● opportunities to relate text to real life events or people, e.g. share the biography of someone familiar and then look at/compare with photos/objects from pupils' own experiences ● selecting stories by relating to props used ● use of photos of pupils with/without family/friends to develop sense of self	*Within an English context pupil remembers learned responses and is pro-active by…* ● glancing alternately at two stimuli ● reacting consistently to the same stimuli ● expressing likes and dislikes consistently ● retaining object momentarily without casting ● making general exploratory movements

English Key Stage: 2
Attainment Target 2: Reading
Key Concept: Pupil should develop visual and auditory awareness through sharing interactive literacy resources

P-Level	Intended Learning Outcomes	Experiences and Activities	Assessment Opportunities

3(i)	**Intentionally Participate**
	
	• with a range of multi-sensory stimuli within an English setting
		Facilitation through an environment which includes the above, plus…
		
		• turn taking within story time
		• encouraging the use of eye pointing, hand reaching for objects and pictures related to the text
		• visits to a bookshop and the school library
		• taking part in drama sessions associated with story
		• holding and referring to artefacts associated with story at appropriate moment
		• making choices within story or song using photo, symbol or object of reference
		• use of communication aids to participate in repeated phrases of text with minimal adult support
		• taking part in actions related to the text
		• encouraging gestural, signing and vocal responses to the text
		• developing use of PECS programmes where pupils are encouraged to identify and share visual cues of preferred motivators
			Within an English context pupil demonstrates an ability to…
			
			• sustain concentration
			• display interested observation, e.g.
			  i) focused looking
			  ii) listening
			  iii) reaching
			
			• make pre verbal communication responses, e.g.
			  i) pointing to objects or events
			  ii) searching for an object after it has 'disappeared'
			  iii) searching for a stimulus after it has stopped
			  iv) choosing to participate (or not)
			  v) seeking attention
			
			• explore in a more diverse way, e.g.
			  i) rubs
			  ii) bangs
			  iii) pushes
			  iv) pulls
			  v) squeezes
			  vi) presses

English Key Stage: 2
Attainment Target 2: Reading
Key Concept: Pupil should develop visual and auditory awareness through sharing interactive literacy resources

P-Level	Intended Learning Outcomes	Experiences and Activities	Assessment Opportunities
3(ii)	**Initiate** • within a range of multi-sensory stimuli in an English setting	*Facilitation through an environment which includes the above, plus…* • initiating/responding to/continuing adult interactions • use of picture sequences to tell story, be it photo, symbol or object of reference • recognising and using artefacts from within story, poem and song • listening to different people read stories • have a reading partner from their peer group with whom they join to share texts on a regular basis • visiting library and/or book shop and choosing books, (could work with reading partner) • matching photos or symbol to picture or object related to the text • use of switches to participate in the right place in the story • developing use of PECS programmes where pupils are encouraged to identify and share visual cues of preferred motivators, and use to initiate responses from peers/staff/family • permanent easy access to photographs of familiar objects and people (for use when initiating interaction/communicating choices)	*Within an English context pupil demonstrates an ability to…* • anticipate known events, follow routines • initiate interactions, activities • actively explore objects/events for more extended periods • take turns in shared activities • use emerging conventional communication by… i) greeting familiar people ii) attempting to sign iii) using symbols iv) recognising photographs v) using objects of reference

English Key Stage: 2
Attainment Target 3: Writing
Key Concept: Pupils should work towards developing fine motor perception skills

P-Level	Intended Learning Outcomes	Experiences and Activities	Assessment Opportunities
1(i)	**Encounter** • a range of multi-sensory stimuli within an English setting	*Facilitation through an environment which includes…* • assistance in manipulating hair gel, mousse, contrasting rough/smooth materials • feeling/exploring personal objects • having hands placed in gloves containing tactile objects • hands placed on sensory objects in support of literacy activities • hands massaged to relax hand and open out fingers • use of individualised tactile artefacts, e.g. cushions with beads, buttons, velvet sewn on, with familiar smell, e.g. Mum's perfume	*Within an English context pupil is present and passive, participation is fully prompted,* *and will make…* • random involuntary movements, e.g. eye flicker, change in body tone
1(ii)	**Awareness of** • a range of multi-sensory stimuli within an English setting	*Facilitation through an environment which includes the above, plus…* • washing hands/feet in different smelling soaps • drying hands with different types of towel: paper, cotton, conti wipe • sensory stimulation using objects/stimuli relating to daily events which pupils experience • being helped to handle different media as part of different lessons • helping pupils to grip and move different objects by developing their tolerance of hand on hand physical support	*Within an English context pupil shows reflex and intermittent reactions, emerging awareness, inconsistent and affective responses by…* • tolerating a range of sensory stimulation: i) tactile ii) auditory iii) visual iv) gustatory v) olfactory vi) kinaesthetic

English Key Stage: 2
Attainment Target 3: Writing
Key Concept: Pupils should work towards developing fine motor perception skills

P-Level	Intended Learning Outcomes	Experiences and Activities	Assessment Opportunities

2(i)	**Respond/React**
	• to a range of multi-sensory stimuli within an English setting
		Facilitation through an environment which includes the above, plus…
		• co-active exploration of household items and harmless foodstuffs
		• opportunities to handle newspapers and magazines
		• using computer programmes such as 'Draw' to encourage pupils to make their own 'stories'
		• being helped to hold/accept a symbol or object of reference and exchange for real object
		• support to make marks in different media: shaving foam, wet cornflour, hair gel, sand, magnetic beads etc.
		• responding to turn taking activities focused on co-active support for hand stretching, reaching, finger movement and other fine motor exercises
			Within an English context pupil shows interest and reactive responses, focused attention and co-actively explores and investigates by…
			• responding to immediate sensory stimulation
			• responding to adult interactions
			• responding when stimulus stops
			• responding to remote sensory stimulation by…
			  i) voluntary movement, e.g. change in facial expression, arm or leg movement
			  ii) eye tracking
			  iii) ear tracking (turns head)
			  iv) vocalising

2(ii)	**Pro-active Co-operation** • within a range of multi-sensory activities and objects within an English setting	*Facilitation through an environment which includes the above, plus…* • opportunities to develop cause and effect, such as using switches with different manual inputs (pad, button, lever etc.) to operate preferred activities, e.g. i) in the sensory room and ii) as integral to focused tasks in the classroom such as preparing dinner • extended opportunities for handling different media, e.g. handcreams • making marks using large pens or brushes on to paper on an angled board • utilising cross-curricular links, e.g. RE/PSHE: painting Mendi patterns with henna on hands to develop sense of self and tolerance of sensation on hands	*Within an English context pupil remembers learned responses and is pro-active by…* • glancing alternately at two stimuli • reacting consistently to the same stimuli • expressing likes and dislikes consistently • retaining object momentarily without casting • making general exploratory movements

English Key Stage: 2
Attainment Target 3: Writing
Key Concept: Pupils should work towards developing fine motor perception skills

P-Level	Intended Learning Outcomes	Experiences and Activities	Assessment Opportunities

3(i)	**Intentionally Participate**
	
	 • with a range of multi-sensory stimuli within an English setting
		Facilitation through an environment which includes the above, plus…
		
		 • turn taking holding and moving hand or arm with large 'scrunchy'
		 • gripping and manipulating interesting, favourite objects
		 • making marks on paper using paints, felt tips, crayons, pencils etc.
		 • moving magnetic letters around on a magnet board
		 • making hand impressions in plaster and rock bandage
		 • putting hands in feely bag to find an object (help may be needed to pull it out)
		 • wearing different textured gloves: gardening, motor bike, sponge mitts, rubber, plastic, glitter etc.
		 • making hand/finger print paintings
			Within an English context pupil demonstrates an ability to…
			
			 • sustain concentration
			 • display interested observation, e.g.
			    i) focused looking
			    ii) listening
			    iii) reaching
			
			 • make pre verbal communication responses, e.g.
			    i) pointing to objects or events
			    ii) searching for an object after it has 'disappeared'
			    iii) searching for a stimulus after it has stopped
			    iv) choosing to participate (or not)
			    v) seeking attention
			
			 • explore in a more diverse way, e.g.
			    i) rubs
			    ii) bangs
			    iii) pushes
			    iv) pulls
			    v) squeezes
			    vi) presses

English Key Stage: 2
Attainment Target 3: Writing
Key Concept: Pupils should work towards developing fine motor perception skills

P-Level	Intended Learning Outcomes	Experiences and Activities	Assessment Opportunities
3(ii)	**Initiate** • within a range of multi-sensory stimuli in an English setting	*Facilitation through an environment which includes the above, plus...* • using hand gestures for communication • picking up objects to look at or feel • taking turns to post items into boxes • using 'Touch Screen' or concept keyboard on computer for cause and effect work • manipulating objects related to interactive literacy activities • manipulating and selecting preferred items • gripping and releasing balls, pens, pegs, rings etc. as requested • extending fingers independently to make marks in sand, cornflour etc.	*Within an English context pupil demonstrates an ability to...* • anticipate known events, follow routines • initiate interactions, activities • actively explore objects/events for more extended periods • take turns in shared activities • use emerging conventional communication by.... i) greeting familiar people ii) attempting to sign iii) using symbols iv) recognising photographs v) using objects of reference

English Key Stage: 3
Attainment Target 1: Speaking & Listening
Key Concept: Pupils should work towards communicating confidently with different people

P-Level	Intended Learning Outcomes	Experiences and Activities	Assessment Opportunities
1(i)	**Encounter** ● a range of multi-sensory stimuli within an English setting	*Facilitation through an environment which includes…* ● adult/peer talking about/referring to specific people and activities associated with the environment as pupils encounter their home or school surroundings ● familiar and unfamiliar people talking through daily routines using photos and objects of reference ● joining a group with unfamiliar people to share in communication, e.g. visiting a café ● meeting visitors and unfamiliar people in a variety of settings ● hearing a range of familiar voices ● being spoken to directly and given an object of reference as a link to the person communicating	*Within an English context pupil is present and passive, participation is fully prompted, and will make…* ● random involuntary movements, e.g. eye flicker, change in body tone
1(ii)	**Awareness of** ● a range of multi-sensory stimuli within an English setting	*Facilitation through an environment which includes the above, plus…* ● ongoing opportunities to hear clear spoken language in preparation for daily activities ● sharing in regular group times with people from community groups ● use of echo mike to promote vocalising and turn taking ● meeting and greeting unfamiliar people in a variety of settings, e.g. Youth Club ● developing awareness of being greeted and welcomed in different settings ● listening to and experiencing drama, talks and regular social visits ● visiting public facilities in the local community: shops, cafés, market, library to communicate to unfamiliar people ● being assisted to use communication aids such as photographs for shopping ● being assisted to maintain a personal timetable to facilitate better awareness of immediate routines, e.g. personal care routine	*Within an English context pupil shows reflex and intermittent reactions, emerging awareness, inconsistent and affective responses by…* ● tolerating a range of sensory stimulation: i) tactile ii) auditory iii) visual iv) gustatory v) olfactory vi) kinaesthetic

English Key Stage: 3
Attainment Target 1: Speaking & Listening
Key Concept: Pupils should work towards communicating confidently with different people

P-Level	Intended Learning Outcomes	Experiences and Activities	Assessment Opportunities
2(i)	**Respond/React** • to a range of multi-sensory stimuli within an English setting	*Facilitation through an environment which includes the above, plus…* • developing personal gestures, sounds for greetings in community settings • being helped to identify and select a wider range of age appropriate activities using photos, objects of reference and sensory cues • being helped to take a more active role in routine class tasks, e.g. having a specific task in group shopping activities • being supported to respond to a wider range of people, especially when out in the community • practice in using photos to make choices when out shopping or in café • having and making regular social visits to provide opportunities for communication • being offered a more active role in art, music and drama workshops • being assisted to maintain a personal timetable to facilitate better awareness of regular routines, e.g. personal care routine	*Within an English context pupil shows interest and reactive responses, focused attention and co-actively explores and investigates by…* • responding to immediate sensory stimulation • responding to adult interactions • responding when stimulus stops • responding to remote sensory stimulation by… i) voluntary movement, e.g. change in facial expression, arm or leg movement ii) eye tracking iii) ear tracking (turns head) iv) vocalising
2(ii)	**Pro-active Co-operation** • within a range of multi-sensory activities and objects within an English setting	*Facilitation through an environment which includes the above, plus…* • use of switches to promote conversations and make one or two word requests in the community • developing and continuing choice-making activities through the use of photos, objects of reference and symbols • helping to maintain a class timetable to facilitate pupils' awareness of daily routines • taking part in activities such as visits to leisure centre, recycling, looking at new building developments etc. so as to become a member of the wider community • developing areas of responsibility within the classroom: being helped to do a class job	*Within an English context pupil remembers learned responses and is pro-active by…* • glancing alternately at two stimuli • reacting consistently to the same stimuli • expressing likes and dislikes consistently • retaining object momentarily without casting • making general exploratory movements

English Key Stage: 3
Attainment Target 1: Speaking & Listening
Key Concept: Pupils should work towards communicating confidently with different people

P-Level	Intended Learning Outcomes	Experiences and Activities	Assessment Opportunities

3(i)	**Intentionally Participate**
	
	• with a range of multi-sensory stimuli within an English setting
		Facilitation through an environment which includes the above, plus…
		
		• use of communication aids with a wider variety of people
		• use of preferred means of communication with familiar and unfamiliar people
		• visiting cafés and other public places and asking for items using communication aids
		• attending shows and venues where public speaking takes place
		• taking part in role play, using speech access devices to address the audience
		• watching different drama productions both within school and out in the theatre
		• working with other people within school on a project and being expected to communicate to them
		• participating with other students in drama activities which reflect real life situations
		• developing areas of responsibility beyond the classroom, i.e. being helped to do a class job which involves activities beyond the classroom
			Within an English context pupil demonstrates an ability to…
			
			• sustain concentration
			• display interested observation, e.g.
			  i) focused looking
			  ii) listening
			  iii) reaching
			
			• make pre verbal communication responses, e.g.
			  i) pointing to objects or events
			  ii) searching for an object after it has 'disappeared'
			  iii) searching for a stimulus after it has stopped
			  iv) choosing to participate (or not)
			  v) seeking attention
			
			• explore in a more diverse way, e.g.
			  i) rubs
			  ii) bangs
			  iii) pushes
			  iv) pulls
			  v) squeezes
			  vi) presses

English Key Stage: 3
Attainment Target 1: Speaking & Listening
Key Concept: Pupils should work towards communicating confidently with different people

P-Level	Intended Learning Outcomes	Experiences and Activities	Assessment Opportunities

3(ii)	• within a range of multi-sensory stimuli in an English setting	*Facilitation through an environment which includes the above, plus…*
		• responding to/continuing adult interactions
		• initiating communication with unfamiliar people both in and out of school using preferred communication method
		• indicating a desire to participate in school activities, e.g. assemblies, visits out in the community, shows etc.
		• participating in questionnaires both in school and out
		• helping to show visitors around school, using communication aids to support interaction
		• being supported to be an active member of a group in school, e.g. Music Group
		• forming links with a group outside of school, e.g. Youth Club
		• being facilitated to make valued contributions to meetings that involve pupils' futures, i.e. reviews
			Within an English context pupil demonstrates an ability to…
			• anticipate known events, follow routines
			• initiate interactions, activities
			• actively explore objects/events for more extended periods
			• take turns in shared activities
			• use emerging conventional communication by…
			  i) greeting familiar people
			  ii) attempting to sign
			  iii) using symbols
			  iv) recognising photographs
			  v) using objects of reference

English Key Stage: 3
Attainment Target 2: Reading
Key Concept: Pupils should develop visual and auditory awareness through sharing interactive literacy resources

P-Level	Intended Learning Outcomes	Experiences and Activities	Assessment Opportunities
1(i)	**Encounter** ● a range of multi-sensory stimuli within an English setting	*Facilitation through an environment which includes…* ● sharing printed images and texts from pupils' immediate surroundings such as adverts, packaging, CD covers, TV, video and computer ● listening to and sharing a variety of stories and texts from different cultures ● being part of a group experiencing stories, poems and songs ● exploring articles related to events within the story ● being supported to hold and explore tactile letters and symbols ● sharing different text genres such as stories from around the world, with linked activities, e.g. tastes/cookery from different countries stories are set in	*Within an English context pupil is present and passive, participation is fully prompted,* *and will make…* ● random involuntary movements, e.g. eye flicker, change in body tone

1(ii)	**Awareness of**
	
	 ● a range of multi-sensory stimuli within an English setting
		Facilitation through an environment which includes the above, plus…
		
		 ● being helped to share a wider range of printed images including photos in newpapapers etc.
		 ● tactile manipulation and sensory exploration of a variety of age appropriate books, magazines, text materials
		 ● hearing language rhythms enhanced with musical instruments/costumes
		 ● opportunities to hear different writers perform their work, e.g. West Indian performance poets on TV, tape etc.
		 ● assisted use of props to support story, poem, song, symbols
		 ● assisted use of switches to access different texts, e.g. 'Big Mac' switch with repeated phrase of story recorded
			Within an English context pupil shows reflex and intermittent reactions, emerging awareness, inconsistent and affective responses by…
			
			 ● tolerating a range of sensory stimulation:
			
			    i) tactile
			    ii) auditory
			    iii) visual
			    iv) gustatory
			    v) olfactory
			    vi) kinaesthetic

English Key Stage: 3
Attainment Target 2: Reading
Key Concept: Pupils should develop visual and auditory awareness through sharing interactive literacy resources

P-Level	Intended Learning Outcomes	Experiences and Activities	Assessment Opportunities
2(i)	**Respond/React** • to a range of multi-sensory stimuli within an English setting	*Facilitation through an environment which includes the above, plus…* • use of props when telling stories to add dimension to the content • hearing different readers engage with texts and having opportunities to respond • use of sensory cues to enhance the experience of the text, including real objects, sounds, smells • seeing key words in the story reading being signed • being assisted to sign key words • being facilitated to make appropriate actions or sounds for characters or events from a range of different texts • exploring environmental symbols through tactile or visual copies of 'men', 'women', road signs, shop logos etc. • developing opportunities to make links between familiar shops and their functions, e.g. letter (parcel): Post Office, groceries: supermarket, etc. • sharing individualised photo albums, which include photos of pupils out in the community	*Within an English context pupil shows interest and reactive responses, focused attention and co-actively explores and investigates by…* • responding to immediate sensory stimulation • responding to adult interactions • responding when stimulus stops • responding to remote sensory stimulation by… i) voluntary movement, e.g. change in facial expression, arm or leg movement ii) eye tracking iii) ear tracking (turns head) iv) vocalising
2(ii)	**Pro-active Co-operation** • within a range of multi-sensory activities and objects within an English setting	*Facilitation through an environment which includes the above, plus…* • use of switches to turn pages of a story on a computer • sharing group reading sessions • working alongside peers to interpret different texts, e.g. reading a recipe • encouraging signing attempts as a response to text, through use of co-active signing • opportunities to link texts to real life, e.g. story from today's newspaper • experiencing texts from around the world; taking part in linked activities • mediating the classroom environment and activities through symbols, tactile and sensory cues • greater use of photos of pupils involved in personal care routines, in order to develop sense of self and opportunities to choose activity and/ or ask for more of an activity, e.g. pupil's hair being brushed, feet being bathed, etc.	*Within an English context pupil shows reflex and intermittent reactions, emerging awareness, inconsistent and affective responses by…* • glancing alternately at two stimuli • reacting consistently to the same stimuli • expressing likes and dislikes consistently • retaining object momentarily without casting • making general exploratory movements

English Key Stage: 3
Attainment Target 2: Reading
Key Concept: Pupils should develop visual and auditory awareness through sharing interactive literacy resources

P-Level	Intended Learning Outcomes	Experiences and Activities	Assessment Opportunities

3(i)	**Intentionally Participate**
	
	● with a range of multi-sensory stimuli within an English setting
		Facilitation through an environment which includes the above, plus…
		
		● taking turns within literacy session
		● access to texts and printed images related to real life, and opportunities to use them, e.g. being helped to select a TV programme from *TV Times*
		● recognising and using the signs and symbols in the local environment
		● displays of common signs from shops, bus stops, public facilities in the class
		● visits to a bookshop, the local library, and newsagents and being expected to express preferences from options given, e.g. select one from two different magazines
		● taking part in drama sessions associated with real life situations, and participating in a wider range of role play situations, e.g. asking for help in the supermarket
		● holding objects associated with stories and texts at appropriate moment
		● making choices using photos, symbol or objects of reference with less adult support
		● use of 'Big Mac' to participate in reading of functional text e.g. recipe, menu
		● developing use of PECS programmes where pupils are encouraged to identify and share visual cues of preferred motivators, including activities in the wider community, e.g. PECS activities focused in a café
			Within an English context pupil demonstrates an ability to…
			
			● sustain concentration
			● display interested observation, e.g.
			  i) focused looking
			  ii) listening
			  iii) reaching
			
			● make pre verbal communication responses, e.g.
			  i) pointing to objects or events
			  ii) searching for an object after it has 'disappeared'
			  iii) searching for a stimulus after it has stopped
			  iv) choosing to participate (or not)
			  v) seeking attention
			
			● explore in a more diverse way, e.g.
			  i) rubs
			  ii) bangs
			  iii) pushes
			  iv) pulls
			  v) squeezes
			  vi) presses

English Key Stage: 3
Attainment Target 2: Reading
Key Concept: Pupils should develop visual and auditory awareness through sharing interactive literacy resources

P-Level	Intended Learning Outcomes	Experiences and Activities	Assessment Opportunities

3(ii)	**Initiate**
	
	• within a range of multi-sensory stimuli in an English setting
		Facilitation through an environment which includes the above, plus…
		
		• initiating/responding to/continuing adult interactions related to texts
		• permanent easy access to photographs of familiar objects and people (for use when initiating interaction/communicating choices)
		• use of picture sequences to organise a task, be it photo, symbol or object of reference, e.g. plan a meal using photos of foods needed
		• use of folk tales, stories related to teenagers, humour, and magazine texts for literacy based activities
		• having access to a range of media, including computer games, CDs etc.
		• listening to different people (familiar and unfamiliar) read stories
		• having a reading partner from pupils' peer group whom they join to share texts on a regular basis
		• visiting newsagents/library/book shop to choose magazine, books (could work with reading partner)
		• on community visits, photograph and observe the signs and symbols in pupils' home surroundings
		• matching photos or symbol to picture or objects related to daily tasks
		• use of PECS programmes where pupils are encouraged to identify and use visual cues of preferred motivators, including activities in the wider community, e.g. PECS activities focused in a café (at 3(ii), pupils to initiate requests/activities)
			Within an English context pupil demonstrates an ability to…
			
			• anticipate known events, follow routines
			• initiate interactions, activities
			• actively explore objects/events for more extended periods
			• take turns in shared activities
			• use emerging conventional communication by…
			  i) greeting familiar people
			  ii) attempting to sign
			  iii) using symbols
			  iv) recognising photographs
			  v) using objects of reference

English Key Stage: 3
Attainment Target 3: Writing
Key Concept: Pupils should work towards developing fine motor perception skills

P-Level	Intended Learning Outcomes	Experiences and Activities	Assessment Opportunities
1(i)	**Encounter** ● a range of multi-sensory stimuli within an English setting	*Facilitation through an environment which includes…* ● assistance in manipulating therapy putty, tactile balls, technology materials (e.g. plastic, wood, metal), natural materials from local environment (e.g. leaves, flowers etc.), food items ● feeling contrasting materials such as CDs, dress fabrics, keys, cuddly toys and other personal objects ● hand massage and stretches ● being helped to feel wet/dry sponges to work on gripping	*Within an English context pupil is present and passive, participation is fully prompted,* *and will make…* ● random involuntary movements, e.g. eye flicker, change in body tone

1(ii)	**Awareness of**
	
	● a range of multi-sensory stimuli within an English setting
		Facilitation through an environment which includes the above, plus…
		
		● developing a fine motor perception and hand skills programme with advice and assistance from the Occupational Therapy and Physiotherapy services
		● use of photos to record daily activities and celebrate achievement
		● being given tactile symbols for an activity to hold until it starts
		● hand and nail care activities
		● experience a professional manicure
			Within an English context pupil shows reflex and intermittent reactions, emerging awareness, inconsistent and affective responses by…
			
			● tolerating a range of sensory stimulation:
			
			   i) tactile
			   ii) auditory
			   iii) visual
			   iv) gustatory
			   v) olfactory
			   vi) kinaesthetic

English Key Stage: 3
Attainment Target 3: Writing
Key Concept: Pupils should work towards developing fine motor perception skills

P-Level	Intended Learning Outcomes	Experiences and Activities	Assessment Opportunities

2(i)	**Respond/React**
	• to a range of multi-sensory stimuli within an English setting
		Facilitation through an environment which includes the above, plus…
		• co-active exploration of household and personal care items
		• drawing attention to hands through use of brightly coloured or scented gloves, noisy wrist bangles
		• help to place hands in oats, seeds, shells, dry pasta; linking to art, food technology and science
		• opportunities to handle comics, books, CDs, magazines
			Within an English context pupil shows interest and reactive responses, focused attention and co-actively explores and investigates by…
			• responding to immediate sensory stimulation
			• responding to adult interactions
			• responding when stimulus stops
			• responding to remote sensory stimulation by…
			  i) voluntary movement, e.g. change in facial expression, arm or leg movement
			  ii) eye tracking
			  iii) ear tracking (turns head)
			  v) vocalising

2(ii)	**Pro-active Co-operation** • within a range of multi-sensory activities and objects within an English setting	*Facilitation through an environment which includes the above, plus…* • co-active work linked to personal care: hand/face washing, tooth brushing • being involved in household tasks such as washing up, preparing food and drinks • access to hand care activities: nail polish, hand creams, nail buffing • switch access to domestic appliances, e.g. food mixer, CD/cassette player for music etc.	*Within an English context pupil remembers learned responses and is pro-active by…* • glancing alternately at two stimuli • reacting consistently to the same stimuli • expressing likes and dislikes consistently • retaining object momentarily without casting • making general exploratory movements

English Key Stage: 3
Attainment Target 3: Writing
Key Concept: Pupils should work towards developing fine motor perception skills

P-Level	Intended Learning Outcomes	Experiences and Activities	Assessment Opportunities

3(i)	**Intentionally Participate**
	
	● with a range of multi-sensory stimuli within an English setting
		Facilitation through an environment which includes the above, plus…
		
		● making marks on paper using paints, felt tips, pen, pencil, chalk
		● use of touch screen to create images on screen with e.g. Dazzle!
		● using drum sticks, guitar, electronic keyboard or drum machine in a music lesson
		● opportunities to explore materials for recycling such as bottles, cans, paper and then take them to be posted in appropriate bins
		● taking part in planting and watering seeds in the school grounds with window boxes and patio pots
		● enjoying a wider range of age appropriate activities focused on developing fine motor perception and manual dexterity, e.g. kneading dough to make bread for the class
			Within an English context pupil demonstrates an ability to…
			
			● sustain concentration
			● display interested observation, e.g.
			  i) focused looking
			  ii) listening
			  iii) reaching
			
			● make pre verbal communication responses, e.g.
			  i) pointing to objects or events
			  ii) searching for an object after it has 'disappeared'
			  iii) searching for a stimulus after it has stopped
			  iv) choosing to participate (or not)
			  v) seeking attention
			
			● explore in a more diverse way, e.g.
			  i) rubs
			  ii) bangs
			  iii) pushes
			  iv) pulls
			  v) squeezes
			  vi) presses

English Key Stage: 3
Attainment Target 3: Writing
Key Concept: Pupils should work towards developing fine motor perception skills

P-Level	Intended Learning Outcomes	Experiences and Activities	Assessment Opportunities

3(ii)	**Initiate**
	• within a range of multi-sensory stimuli in an English setting
		Facilitation through an environment which includes the above, plus…
		• being helped to write/contribute to greetings cards
		• placing thumb/finger print on notes, thank you letters, letters home, invitations
		• participating in computer tasks using symbolised programs and concept keyboard with key words on it, such as Inclusive Writer (e.g. to make a shopping list for the class)
		• painting with large brushes, rollers, sponges on sticks
		• shaving practice for boys using a face massager
			Within an English context pupil demonstrates an ability to…
			• anticipate known events, follow routines
			• initiate interactions, activities
			• actively explore objects/events for more extended periods
			• take turns in shared activities
			• use emerging conventional communication by…
			  i) greeting familiar people
			  ii) attempting to sign
			  iii) using symbols
			  iv) recognising photographs
			  v) using objects of reference

Mathematics

Mathematics Key Stage: 1
Number: Using & Applying
Shape, Space & Measure: Using & Applying

P-Level	Intended Learning Outcomes	Experiences & Activities for Number	Experiences & Activities for Shape, Space & Measure	Assessment Opportunities
1(i)	**Encounter** • a range of multi-sensory stimuli within a mathematical context	*Facilitation through an environment which includes…* • counting numbers, use of the correct language and vocabulary associated with number and data • singing number action rhymes with props, e.g. '5 Little Speckled Frogs' • fully prompted sensory exploration of tactile numerals, and objects relating to themselves, e.g. near person objects of reference and age appropriate stimuli • body patting numbers • physio or rhythmical movement which incorporates counting and develops anticipation • number stories, e.g. 'Spot can Count'	*Facilitation through an environment which includes…* • exploration of tactile shapes • exploration of shapes with contrasting attributes, e.g. long/short, big/small • attribute stories, e.g. 'Whatever next?' • whole body experiences, e.g. use of balloons and sensory balls • fully supported movement to LDA body awareness tapes	*Within a mathematical context pupil is present and outwardly passive, participation is fully prompted* and will make… • random involuntary movements, e.g. eye flicker, change in body tone
1(ii)	**Awareness of** • a range of multi-sensory stimuli within a mathematical context	*Facilitation through an environment which includes the above, plus…* • number mobiles • sensory stimulation using objects/stimuli relating to themselves, e.g. 'Big Mac' switch with familiar recorded sound • visual representations of numerals • use of switches to access relevant software, e.g. 'Switch On!'	*Facilitation through an environment which includes the above, plus…* • sharing a range of soft shapes, e.g. balls with bells in • activities which promote body awareness • use of switches to activate shape stimulus/reward • sand and water activities • activities using the ball pool	*Within a mathematical context pupil shows reflex and intermittent reactions, emerging awareness, inconsistent and affective responses by…* • accepting a range of sensory stimulation: i) tactile ii) auditory iii) visual iv) gustatory v) olfactory vi) kinaesthetic

Mathematics Key Stage: 1
Number: Using & Applying
Shape, Space & Measure: Using & Applying

P-Level	Intended Learning Outcomes	Experiences & Activities for Number	Experiences & Activities for Shape, Space & Measure	Assessment Opportunities
2(i)	**Respond/React** • to a range of multi-sensory stimuli within a mathematical context	*Facilitation through an environment which includes the above, plus…* • co-active exploration of a range of stimuli including individualised / personalised resources, e.g. teddy bears, noisy toys etc. • use of sensory room to illustrate number songs, rhymes etc. • use of switches to access a range of appropriate maths software, e.g. 'Brilliant' • number games using puppets	*Facilitation through an environment which includes the above, plus…* • co-active exploration of a range of sensory or tactile shapes • bubble painting • shape mobiles • making shapes using own body • co-active exploration of soft play shapes • Jack-in-the-box!	*Within a mathematical context pupil shows interest and reactive responses, focused attention and co-actively explores and investigates by…* • responding to immediate sensory stimulation • responding to adult interactions • responding when stimulus stops • responding to remote sensory stimulation by… i) voluntary movement e.g. change in facial expression, arm or leg movement ii) eye tracking iii) ear tracking (turns head) iv) vocalising
2(ii)	**Pro-active Co-operation** • within a range of multi-sensory activities and objects within a mathematical context	*Facilitation through an environment which includes the above, plus…* • opportunities to develop the concept of more or repetition of an activity • tracing numerals in tactile media, e.g. cornflour, sand • making towers with giant soft bricks and then knocking them down • helping to assemble train track and anticipating trains passing • developing turn taking through partner games	*Facilitation through an environment which includes the above, plus…* • co-active participation in stacking rings, posting boxes, etc. • transparent container play • hiding 3D shapes in sand • printing patterns with feet and hands	*Within a mathematical context pupil remembers learned responses and is pro-active by…* • glancing alternately at two stimuli • reacting consistently to the same stimuli • expressing likes and dislikes consistently • retaining object momentarily without casting • making general exploratory movements

Mathematics Key Stage: 1
Number: Using & Applying
Shape, Space & Measure: Using & Applying

P-Level	Intended Learning Outcomes	Experiences & Activities for Number	Experiences & Activities for Shape, Space & Measure	Assessment Opportunities

3(i)	**Intentionally Participate**
	
	 ● with a range of multi-sensory stimuli within a mathematical context
		Facilitation through an environment which includes the above, plus...
		
		 ● turn taking games, e.g. 'Pass the Hat'
		 ● removing or adding props during counting rhymes
		 ● opportunities to develop anticipation in number games, e.g. 1, 2, 3 ... Go!
		 ● posting tactile numbers
			Facilitation through an environment which includes the above, plus...
			
			 ● mirror games
			 ● printing patterns with hands and feet
			 ● junk modelling
				Within a mathematical context pupil demonstrates an ability to...
				
				 ● sustain concentration
				 ● display interested observation, e.g.
				   i) focused looking
				   ii) listening
				   iii) reaching
				
				 ● make pre-verbal communication responses, e.g.
				   i) pointing to objects or events
				   ii) searching for an object after it has 'disappeared'
				   iii) searching for a stimulus after it has stopped
				   iv) choosing to participate (or not)
				   v) seeking attention
				
				 ● explore in a more diverse way, e.g.
				   i) rubs
				   ii) bangs
				   iii) pushes
				   iv) pulls
				   v) squeezes
				   vi) presses

Mathematics Key Stage: 1
Number: Using & Applying
Shape, Space & Measure: Using & Applying

P-Level	Intended Learning Outcomes	Experiences & Activities for Number	Experiences & Activities for Shape, Space & Measure	Assessment Opportunities

3(ii)	**Initiate**
	
	• within a range of multi-sensory stimuli in a mathematical context
		Facilitation through an environment which includes the above, plus…
		
		• building a brick tower in response to a counting rhyme
		• developing partner games
		• following musical patterns
		• opportunities to predict and effect regular events by making associations within daily routines, e.g. coat = going out; tape/CD = music
			Facilitation through an environment which includes the above plus…
			
			• action stories, e.g. time: 'Peace at Last', 'Hickory Dickory Dock' shape: 'Whatever Next' colour: 'Elmer' size: 'Where's my Teddy?'
			• joining in with action rhymes
			• hide and seek games, e.g. pulling off a cloth to reveal…
			• mirror games
				Within a mathematical context pupil demonstrates an ability to…
				
				• anticipate known events, follow routines
				• initiate interactions, activities
				• actively explore objects/events for more extended periods
				• take turns in shared activities
				• use emerging conventional communication by…
				  i) greeting familiar people
				  ii) attempting to sign
				  iii) using symbols
				  iv) recognising photographs
				  v) using objects of reference

Mathematics Key Stage: 2
Number: Using & Applying
Shape, Space & Measure: Using & Applying

P-Level	Intended Learning Outcomes	Experiences & Activities for Number	Experiences & Activities for Shape, Space & Measure	Assessment Opportunities
1(i)	**Encounter** • a range of multi-sensory stimuli within a mathematical context	*Facilitation through an environment which includes…* • counting numbers, use of the correct language and vocabulary associated with number and data • singing number action rhymes with props, e.g. '5 Little Speckled Frogs' • fully prompted sensory exploration of classroom objects, e.g. cups for drinks • body patting numbers • number stories, e.g. 'Splash!' and '1, 2, 3 Off to the Sea'	*Facilitation through an environment which includes…* • exploration of tactile shapes within a sensory medium, e.g. spheres in jelly • attribute stories, e.g. 'Dinosaur Roar'	*Within a mathematical context pupil is present and outwardly passive, participation is fully prompted,* and will make… • random involuntary movements, e.g. eye flicker, change in body tone
1(ii)	**Awareness of** • a range of multi-sensory stimuli within a mathematical context	*Facilitation through an environment which includes the above, plus…* • age appropriate sensory representation of numerals, e.g. jellies made in number moulds • 'jungle maths'… beat out numbers on drums • use of switches to access relevant software, e.g. 'Switch On', also touch games such as 'Rocket'	*Facilitation through an environment which includes the above, plus…* • sharing a range of soft shapes, e.g. balls with bells in • age appropriate activities which promote body awareness • use of switches to activate shape stimulus/reward	*Within a mathematical context pupil shows reflex and intermittent reactions, emerging awareness, inconsistent and affective responses by…* • accepting a range of sensory stimulation: i) tactile ii) auditory iii) visual iv) gustatory v) olfactory vi) kinaesthetic

Mathematics Key Stage: 2
Number: Using & Applying
Shape, Space & Measure: Using & Applying

P-Level	Intended Learning Outcomes	Experiences & Activities for Number	Experiences & Activities for Shape, Space & Measure	Assessment Opportunities

2(i)	**Respond/React**
	• to a range of multi-sensory stimuli within a mathematical context
		Facilitation through an environment which includes the above, plus…
		• co-active exploration of a range of stimuli including individualised / personalised resources, e.g. favourite item
		• physical patterning activities from Waldon approach, e.g. brick building with numbers
		• use of tactile gloves, e.g. brightly coloured fabric with bells on and fluorescent gloves for counting under UV in the sensory room
		• puppet games
		• number mobiles
			Facilitation through an environment which includes the above, plus…
			• co-active exploration of a range of sensory or tactile shapes
			• shape mobiles
			• painting hands and faces with patterns
			• use of 'soundbeam' to support co-active exploration
				Within a mathematical context pupil shows interest and reactive responses, focused attention and co-actively explores and investigates by…
				• responding to immediate sensory stimulation
				• responding to adult interactions
				• responding when stimulus stops
				• responding to remote sensory stimulation by…
				  i) voluntary movement, e.g. change in facial expression, arm or leg movement
				  ii) eye tracking
				  iii) ear tracking (turns head)
				  iv) vocalising

2(ii)	**Pro-active Co-operation** • within a range of multi-sensory activities and objects within a mathematical context	*Facilitation through an environment which includes the above, plus…* • partner games • hide and seek-type games • posting tactile numbers • counting beats using percussion	*Facilitation through an environment which includes the above, plus…* • co-active exploration of long-short, big-small, heavy-light • co-active exploration of a range of shapes and changing shapes in clay/dough • printing shape sequences	*Within a mathematical context pupil remembers learned responses and is pro-active by…* • glancing alternately at two stimuli • reacting consistently to the same stimuli • expressing likes and dislikes consistently • retaining object momentarily without casting • making general exploratory movements

Mathematics Key Stage: 2
Number: Using & Applying
Shape, Space & Measure: Using & Applying

P-Level	Intended Learning Outcomes	Experiences & Activities for Number	Experiences & Activities for Shape, Space & Measure	Assessment Opportunities

3(i)	**Intentionally Participate**
	
	 • with a range of multi-sensory stimuli within a mathematical context
		Facilitation through an environment which includes the above, plus…
		
		 • turn-taking games such as passing the 'feely' bag
		 • finding a number of items hidden in a sensory medium
			Facilitation through an environment which includes the above, plus…
			
			 • mirror games
			 • use of chime bars or wood blocks to strike out repeating patterns
				Within a mathematical context pupil demonstrates an ability to…
				
				 • sustain concentration
				 • display interested observation, e.g.
				  i) focused looking
				  ii) listening
				  iii) reaching
				
				 • pre-verbal communication responses, e.g.
				  i) pointing to objects or events
				  ii) searching for an object after it has 'disappeared'
				  iii) searching for a stimulus after it has stopped
				  iv) choosing to participate (or not)
				  v) seeking attention
				
				 • explore in a more diverse way, e.g.
				  i) rubs
				  ii) bangs
				  iii) pushes
				  iv) pulls
				  v) squeezes
				  vi) presses

Mathematics Key Stage: 2
Number: Using & Applying
Shape, Space & Measure: Using & Applying

P-Level	Intended Learning Outcomes	Experiences & Activities for Number	Experiences & Activities for Shape, Space & Measure	Assessment Opportunities
3(ii)	**Initiate** • within a range of multi-sensory stimuli in a mathematical context	*Facilitation through an environment which includes the above, plus…* • use of switches to access a range of appropriate maths software, e.g. 'Count!' • using 'Big Mac' switch to join in counting rhymes and games	*Facilitation through an environment which includes the above, plus…* • action stories, e.g. time: 'Mr Wolf's Week' shape: 'Blue Balloon' colour: 'Rainbow Bear' size: 'The Enormous Turnip'	*Within a mathematical context pupil demonstrates an ability to…* • anticipate known events, follow routines • initiate interactions, activities • actively explore objects/events for more extended periods • take turns in shared activities • use emerging conventional communication by… i) greeting familiar people ii) attempting to sign iii) using symbols iv) recognising photographs v) using objects of reference

Mathematics Key Stage: 3
Number: Using & Applying
Shape, Space & Measure: Using & Applying

P-Level	Intended Learning Outcomes	Experiences & Activities for Number	Experiences & Activities for Shape, Space & Measure	Assessment Opportunities
1(i)	**Encounter** • a range of multi-sensory stimuli within a mathematical setting	*Facilitation through an environment which includes…* • counting numbers, use of the correct language and vocabulary associated with number and data • singing number songs with props, e.g. 'Alice the Camel' • fully prompted sensory exploration of classroom objects • number stories, e.g. 'Noah'	*Facilitation through an environment which includes…* • exploration of tactile 3D shapes and real life objects such as packaging • attribute paintings, e.g. Picasso or cubism	*Within a mathematical context pupil is present and outwardly passive, participation is fully prompted,* and will make… • random involuntary movements, e.g. eye flicker, change in body tone
1(ii)	**Awareness of** • a range of multi-sensory stimuli within a mathematical context	*Facilitation through an environment which includes the above, plus…* • icing numbers on cakes or biscuits • world maths… beat out numbers on drums, tubular bells • switch access to a range of software which promotes cause and effect, e.g. 'Out & About', 'Streetwise', 'Animated Numbers'	*Facilitation through an environment which includes the above, plus…* • sharing a range of soft shapes, e.g. balls with bells in • activities which promote body awareness • use of switches to activate shape stimulus/reward • coloured cellophane hoops • shape mobiles	*Within a mathematical context pupil shows reflex and intermittent reactions, emerging awareness, inconsistent and affective responses by…* • accepting a range of sensory stimulation: i) tactile ii) auditory iii) visual iv) gustatory v) olfactory vi) kinaesthetic

Mathematics Key Stage: 3
Number: Using & Applying
Shape, Space & Measure: Using & Applying

P-Level	Intended Learning Outcomes	Experiences & Activities for Number	Experiences & Activities for Shape, Space & Measure	Assessment Opportunities
2(i)	**Respond/React** • to a range of multi-sensory stimuli within a mathematical context	*Facilitation through an environment which includes the above, plus...* • co-active exploration of a range of stimuli including individualised/personalised resources, e.g. favourite item • tracing numbers in a tactile medium • making number displays using refractive paper • use switches to access a range of age appropriate maths software • use tactile, or fluorescent gloves for counting • count colour co-ordinated clothing • number mobiles, e.g. money • use bendy light tubes to make numbers in sensory room	*Facilitation through an environment which includes the above, plus...* • co-active exploration of a range of sensory or tactile shapes • experience shapes in the environment, windows, doors, plates • paint hands and faces with patterns • shape patterns, food packets • use 'Soundbeam' for co-active exploration	*Within a mathematical context pupil shows interest and reactive responses, focused attention and co-actively explores and investigates by...* • responding to immediate sensory stimulation • responding to adult interactions • responding when stimulus stops • responding to remote sensory stimulation by... i) voluntary movement, e.g. change in facial expression, arm or leg movement ii) eye tracking iii) ear tracking (turns head) iv) vocalising
2(ii)	**Pro-active Co-operation** • within a range of multi-sensory activities and objects within a mathematical context	*Facilitation through an environment which includes the above, plus...* • age appropriate partner games • compare clothing sizes • post tactile numbers • paint nails... count fingers • move students along a number line • look at numbers in the environment, e.g. phone numbers, house numbers	*Facilitation through an environment which includes the above, plus...* • link food with packets, e.g. Toblerone, Pringles • parachute games • make biscuits with shape cutters	*Within a mathematical context pupil remembers learned responses and is pro-active by...* • glancing alternately at two stimuli • reacting consistently to the same stimuli • expressing likes and dislikes consistently • retaining object momentarily without casting • making general exploratory movements

Mathematics Key Stage: 3
Number: Using & Applying
Shape, Space & Measure: Using & Applying

P-Level	Intended Learning Outcomes	Experiences & Activities for Number	Experiences & Activities for Shape, Space & Measure	Assessment Opportunities
3(i)	**Intentionally Participate** • with a range of multi-sensory stimuli within a mathematical context	*Facilitation through an environment which includes the above, plus…* • turn-taking games such as passing the 'feely' bag • skittles/boules • leisure activities relating to number, e.g. pressing numbers on a TV remote control • dance to disco… move to the music… feel the beat	*Facilitation through an environment which includes the above, plus…* • mirror games • news stories… time: 'Today's Headlines' shape: 'Clothing Styles' colour: fabric swatches colour co-ordination in clothing fashions • make and use kites on a windy day • printing patterns, make wallpaper designs • shapes in World stories, e.g. fruit in 'Handa's Surprise', houses in 'The story of the round house and the square house'	*Within a mathematical context pupil demonstrates an ability to…* • sustain concentration • display interested observation, e.g. i) focused looking ii) listening iii) reaching • make pre verbal communication responses, e.g. i) pointing to objects or events ii) searching for an object after it has 'disappeared' iii) searching for a stimulus after it has stopped iv) choosing to participate (or not) v) seeking attention • explore in a more diverse way, e.g. i) rubs ii) bangs iii) pushes iv) pulls v) squeezes vi) presses

Mathematics Key Stage: 3
Number: Using & Applying
Shape, Space & Measure: Using & Applying

P-Level	Intended Learning Outcomes	Experiences & Activities for Number	Experiences & Activities for Shape, Space & Measure	Assessment Opportunities
3(ii)	**Initiate** • within a range of multi-sensory stimuli in a mathematical context	*Facilitation through an environment which includes the above, plus…* • respond to/continue adult interactions • exploratory actions to recreate effect, e.g. use switch to turn fan on • combine objects for a purpose, e.g. stir drink with spoon • develop object use and its associations, e.g. cup = drink, coat = going out • anticipate the path of a moving object • explore the third dimension of objects, prod or poke new items in class • water and container activities, e.g. washing up	*Facilitation through an environment which includes the above, plus…* • post a letter • place a cassette in tape recorder • put bread in toaster	*Within a mathematical context pupil demonstrates an ability to…* • anticipate known events, follow routines • initiate interactions, activities • actively explore objects/events for more extended periods • take turns in shared activities • use emerging conventional communication by… i) greeting familiar people ii) attempting to sign iii) using symbols iv) recognising photographs v) using objects of reference

Science

Science Key Stage: 1
Attainment Target 1: Scientific Enquiry
Investigative Skills

P-Level	Intended Learning Outcomes	Experiences and Activities for Scientific Enquiry	Assessment Opportunities
1(i)	**Encounter** • a range of multi-sensory stimuli within a scientific context	*Facilitated through learning activities which provide experience of…* • the sensory properties (smell, texture, visual aspects) of kinaesthetic reactions to familiar and unfamiliar objects such as: soap and sand, water and bubble mixture, own favourite toys and new toys • the sensory properties of man-made and natural items such as: wooden, fabric and plastic toys; their own and other people's arms, legs, hands, feet, facial features and hair • the sensory properties of gases, liquids, and solids: the feel and sound of the air moving when somebody gently blows on them, the stream of air from a hairdryer; the feel and sound of moving water; the sensory properties of construction blocks loose and when fitted together • a variety of whole body movements: swinging in a blanket and in a swing seat, travelling on a roundabout, going down a slide, rocking on a rocking horse or on a rocking board • a variety of temperatures through: water play activities using warm and cool water, lying on a heated waterbed or on the cool floor, encountering warm and cool air from the hairdryer, encountering warm play dough and play dough from the fridge • a variety of light intensities, colours and movement: daylight, dappled shade, black and white mobiles, finger puppets under UV light, light reflected off a survival blanket	*Within the scientific context pupil is present and outwardly passive, participation is fully prompted.* Pupil may… • make random involuntary movement, e.g. eye flicker • show change in body tone • show change in breathing rate/depth

1(ii)	**Awareness of**
	
	 • a range of multi-sensory stimuli within a scientific context
		Facilitated through learning activities which provide experience of the above, as well as activities that provide, within each sensory modality, similar/contrasting sensations such as…
		
		 • being touched on arms, legs, hands, feet with different textures: sheepskin, dish mop, sponge, netting, cotton wool, sun cream, aromatherapy/massage oils
		 • being provided with different sounds to listen to: live or recorded nursery songs, sound producing toys, story tapes, sound lotto, percussion and tuned instruments, theme tunes to children's TV programmes, the voices of familiar and unfamiliar adults and children
		 • being provided with visually stimulating environment including; coloured and black and white patterned mobiles, flashing and coloured Christmas lights; working under UV lights, on a reflective surface
			Within the scientific context pupil shows reflex and intermittent reactions, emerging awareness, inconsistent and affective responses…
			
			 • Pupils may tolerate a range of sensory stimulation:
			   i) tactile
			   ii) auditory
			   iii) visual
			   iv) gustatory
			   v) olfactory
			   vi) kinaesthetic

Science Key Stage: 1
Attainment Target 1: Scientific Enquiry
Investigative Skills

P-Level	Intended Learning Outcomes	Experiences and Activities for Scientific Enquiry	Assessment Opportunities

2(i)	**Respond/React**
	
	• to a range of multi-sensory stimuli within a scientific context
		Facilitated through learning activities which includes the above, as well as activities which provide opportunities to co-actively…
		
		• explore using all available senses, objects with a range of similar/contrasting properties: household shopping such as egg box, cereal box, pack of dried fruit, tin of beans/dried milk, carton of juice, bananas, frozen peas
		• make percussion instruments such as 'open' shakers using wide necked pots or tins containing peas, sand, cotton wool, marbles etc. which can be played by stirring around with the hand
		• respond to the effect produced when assisted to operate cause and effect equipment: switch operated computer programme, switch operated grunting toy pig, train set
		• respond to; the start/finish of action songs and games, finger rhymes; the change in light intensity when a light is turned on/off; bubbles floating by and popping; the action of pop-up toys such as a Jack-in-the-box
			Within the scientific context pupil shows interest.
			
			Pupil may…
			
			• respond to the start/finish of proximal sensory stimulation
			• respond to adult/peer interaction
			• respond to start/finish of distal sensory stimulation
			• begin to react consistently, indicative of a 'like' or 'don't like' response to given stimuli
			
			Pupil's response may be indicated by….
			  i) voluntary movement, e.g. change in facial expression
			  ii) arm or leg movement
			  iii) eye tracking
			  iv) ear tracking (turns head)
			  v) vocalisation

Science Key Stage: 1
Attainment Target 1: Scientific Enquiry
Investigative Skills

P-Level	Intended Learning Outcomes	Experiences and Activities for Scientific Enquiry	Assessment Opportunities
2(ii)	**Pro-active Co-operation** • within a range of multi-sensory activities and with objects within a scientific context	*Facilitated through learning activities which include the above, as well as activities which provide opportunities to pro-actively…* • explore using all available senses, objects and environments such as a familiar adult's facial features; parts of their own body; their own face in a mirror; elements of a mobile; toys in a toy box • communicate preferences between: tastes and textures of food and drink; toys, colours of lights, people, tactile experiences such as water and sand play, play dough and finger painting; experiences of massage with sheepskin, sponge, netting on arms, legs, hands, feet • assist, by giving differential responses, with grouping objects: soft toys/hard toys, reflective/non-reflective surfaces, objects producing high tones/low tones	*Within the scientific context pupil remembers learned responses and is pro-active.* Pupil may… • glance alternately at two stimuli • react consistently to the same stimuli • express likes and dislikes consistently • retain object momentarily without casting • make general exploratory movements

Science Key Stage: 1
Attainment Target 1: Scientific Enquiry
Investigative Skills

P-Level	Intended Learning Outcomes	Experiences and Activities for Scientific Enquiry	Assessment Opportunities

3(i)	**Intentionally Participate**
	
	● with a range of multi-sensory stimuli within a scientific context
		Facilitated through learning activities which include the above, as well as activities which provide opportunities to…
		
		independently using available senses, investigate items within their environment such as:
		
		● search for a favourite toy in toy box, move head/eyes to find 'missing' bubbles when they pop, move head to locate a sound, search for shapes inside posting box after being helped to post them
		● participate in, or deliberately choose not to participate in: Peek-a-boo and Hide-and-seek games, action songs and rhymes, 'Pass the Parcel', possibly by visually tracking the parcel as it moves around the group
		● act on objects in a variety of ways: poke and squeeze wet sand, bang and shake toys, reach and knock hanging mobiles, visually scan changes in environment such as adult's new hair style, pull toy across table, track movement of wind-up toy
			Within the scientific context pupil may demonstrate an ability to…
			
			● sustain concentration
			● display interested observation
			  i) focused looking
			  ii) focused listening
			  iii) reaching
			● communicate preverbally using physical, vocal, auditory or visual skills by:
			  i) pointing to objects or events
			  ii) searching for an object after it has 'disappeared'
			  iii) searching for a stimulus after it has stopped
			  iv) choosing or refusing to participate
			  v) seeking attention
			● explore in more diverse ways
			  i) rubs
			  ii) bangs
			  iii) pushes
			  iv) pulls
			  v) squeezes
			  vi) presses
			  vii) scans
			  viii) tracks

Science Key Stage: 1
Attainment Target 1: Scientific Enquiry
Investigative Skills

P-Level	Intended Learning Outcomes	Experiences and Activities for Scientific Enquiry	Assessment Opportunities
3(ii)	**Initiate** ● with a range of multi-sensory stimuli within a scientific context	*Facilitated through learning activities which include the above, as well as activities which provide opportunities to…* ● participate in turn-taking games: giving and taking a toy, rolling a ball, splashing in water, looking at partner and smiling, clapping games and songs ● purposefully investigate objects/features in the environment such as by: searching for a 'noisy' toy by shaking and discarding toys from a selection until one is found which will rattle; holding and turning items to find one which reflects the light ● anticipate: a sound when a toy falls and lands on the floor, the cold when offered ice cream, movement when sitting on a swing ● purposely explore the units of construction kits, attempting to put them together/take them apart	*Within the scientific context pupil may demonstrate an ability to…* ● anticipate known events, follow routines ● initiate interactions, activities ● actively explore objects/events for more extended periods ● take turns in shared activities ● use emerging conventional communication by… 　i) greeting familiar people 　ii) attempting to sign 　iii) using symbols 　iv) recognising photographs 　v) using objects of reference 　vi) eye-pointing 　vii) using PECS (Pictorial Exchange Communication System)

Science Key Stage: 2
Attainment Target 1: Scientific Enquiry
Investigative Skills

P-Level	Intended Learning Outcomes	Experiences and Activities for Investigative Skills	Assessment Opportunities
1(i)	**Encounter** • a range of multi-sensory stimuli within a scientific context	*Facilitated through learning activities which provide experience of…* • the sensory properties (smell, texture, visual aspects) of kinaesthetic reaction to familiar and unfamiliar objects such as: sandpaper, wrapping paper, magazines, tissue paper, tin foil, cling film • the sensory properties of man-made and natural items such as: plastic bottles, cardboard tubes, packaging and bubble wrap as well as stones, leaves, plants and domestic animals • the sensory properties of gases, liquids, and solids, e.g. the wind, moving air from a fan, water, papier maché paste; a variety of food technology ingredients; whole, juiced and pureed fruit and vegetables, uncooked ingredients for bread and cooked bread as well as the experience of lying on loosely or tightly packed balls in a ball pool • a variety of whole body movements including: swinging in a wheelchair user's swing, riding on a pony or in a pony and trap, floating on a lilo, floating with arm bands, lying on a bouncy castle and in a ball pool as well as experiencing changes in speed and direction when 'wheelchair dancing' or playing 'wheelchair tag' • a variety of temperatures through experience of: a heated hydrotherapy pool and local swimming pool; food technology activities requiring access to a fridge or warm oven; encountering 'warm' materials, e.g. fur fabric, polystyrene and 'cool' materials such as satin, slate; experiencing cold frosty days and warm, sunny days • a variety of light intensities, colours and movement such as those provided by: lights in the Sensory Room or Snoozlem, fish in a fish tank, the flashing lights on electronic toys and games, holographic paper, Christmas decorations	*Within the scientific context pupil is present and outwardly passive, participation is fully prompted.* Pupil may… • make random involuntary movement e.g. eye flicker • show change in body tone • show change in breathing rate/depth

Science Key Stage: 2
Attainment Target 1: Scientific Enquiry
Investigative Skills

P-Level	Intended Learning Outcomes	Experiences and Activities for Investigative Skills	Assessment Opportunities
		Facilitated through learning activities which provide experience of the above, as well as activities that provide, within each sensory modality, similar/contrasting sensations such as…	*Within the scientific context pupil shows reflex and intermittent reactions, emerging awareness, inconsistent and affective responses.*

1(ii)	**Awareness of**
	
	• a range of multi-sensory stimuli within a scientific context
		• being touched on arms, legs, hands, feet, face with: bubble wrap and other packaging materials; empty plastic bottles, art stippling brushes, paint rollers
		• being played different types of music and sounds: pop songs and classical music, new age music, radio, book and poetry tapes, recorded familiar voices and own voice as well as live music such as being played/sung to by visiting musicians or at a pantomime
		• having face, hands, objects draped in transparent, translucent and opaque fabrics; working with mirrors and objects with reflective surfaces
			Pupil may…
			
			• tolerate a range of sensory stimulation:
			  i) tactile
			  ii) auditory
			  iii) visual
			  iv) gustatory
			  v) olfactory
			  vi) kinaesthetic

Science Key Stage: 2
Attainment Target 1: Scientific Enquiry
Investigative Skills

P-Level	Intended Learning Outcomes	Experiences and Activities for Investigative Skills	Assessment Opportunities
2(i)	**Respond/React** • to a range of multi-sensory stimuli within a scientific context	*Facilitated through learning activities which include the above, as well as activities which provide opportunities to co-actively...* • explore using all available senses, objects with a range of contrasting/similar properties such as items linked to a class project; dried and fresh leaves, trunks of living trees, fresh herbs, sawdust, wood shavings, sawn timber • make different sounds by hitting objects with different surfaces such as: a drum, pillow, a person's hand or tray • respond to the effect produced when assisted to operate cause and effect equipment, e.g. switch operated fan, electronic organ, toy robot or when helped to roll a ball down a ramp or move marbles around a tray • respond to the different smells/sounds/sights encountered in a farmyard/park/school • respond to the visual stimulus provided by: pop-up books, action figures and toys which move as well as the movement of light such as torchlight when shone directly onto own body or through translucent fabrics or when reflected off mirrors	*Within the scientific context pupil shows interest.* Pupil may... • respond to the start/finish of proximal sensory stimulation • respond to adult/peer interaction • respond to start/finish of distal sensory stimulation • begin to react consistently indicative of a 'like' or 'don't like' response to given stimuli Pupil's response may be indicated by... i) voluntary movement, e.g. change in facial expression ii) arm or leg movement iii) eye tracking iv) ear tracking (turns head) v) vocalisation

Science Key Stage: 2
Attainment Target 1: Scientific Enquiry
Investigative Skills

P-Level	Intended Learning Outcomes	Experiences and Activities for Investigative Skills	Assessment Opportunities
2(ii)	**Proactive Co-operation** • within a range of multi-sensory activities and with objects within a scientific context	*Facilitated through learning activities which include the above as well as activities which provide opportunities to pro-actively…* • explore using all available senses, objects and environments such as: other people's facial features, parts of their peers' or friends' bodies including hands and hair; their own bodies in a mirror, perhaps by matching their hands to the reflection on a mirror as well as objects such as: flour or water – filled balloons, clay • communicate preferences including: tastes and textures of food and drink, colours of lights, preferred sounds such as mum's voice or favourite pop group recorded on a 'Big Mac' switch; tactile experiences such as sensory hand, foot, finger painting as well as experiences of massage with sheepskin, sponge, netting on arms, legs, hands, feet • develop understanding of cause and effect for example through switch work with equipment in the sensory room • assist, by giving differential response, with the sorting out of collections of items: soft foods from hard, reflective items from non-reflective, flexible materials from rigid	*Within the scientific context pupil remembers learned responses and is pro-active.* Pupil may… • glance alternately at two stimuli • react consistently to the same stimuli • express likes and dislikes consistently • retain object momentarily without casting • make general exploratory movements

Science Key Stage: 2
Attainment Target 1: Scientific Enquiry
Investigative Skills

P-Level	Intended Learning Outcomes	Experiences and Activities for Investigative Skills	Assessment Opportunities
3(i)	**Intentionally Participate**	*Facilitated through activities which include the above, as well as activities which provide opportunities to…*	*Within the scientific context pupil may demonstrate an ability to…*
	• with a range of multi-sensory stimuli within a scientific context	independently, using available senses, investigate items within their environment such as:	• sustain concentration
			• display interested observation
		• participate in, or deliberately choose not to participate in: group/paired activities such as; pushing balls across a table, 'playing' percussion instruments, splashing in water, stilling and listening carefully during auditory activities such as 'Sound Lotto'	i) focused looking
			ii) focused listening
			iii) reaching
		• act on objects in a variety of ways: crumple or pull to tear newspaper, bubble wrap, tissue paper and card; randomly squeeze and push construction equipment together; grasp and crush handfuls of cornflakes, sawdust; pull fabrics over own or adult's face or hands	• communicate pre verbally using physical, vocal, auditory or visual skills by:
			i) pointing to objects or events
		• search for preferred percussion instrument from a selection; search for an accidentally dropped ball; explore container after posting object into it	ii) searching for an object after it has 'disappeared'
		• look at objects through visual equipment/apparatus: look at own hands or at friends' faces through a magnifying glass; look at people and faces in convex/concave mirrors; look at familiar objects through different coloured lenses	iii) searching for a stimulus after it has stopped
			iv) choosing or refusing to participate
			v) seeking attention
			• explore in more diverse way
			i) rubs
			ii) bangs
			iii) pushes
			iv) pulls
			v) squeezes
			vi) presses
			vii) scans
			viii) tracks

Science Key Stage: 2
Attainment Target 1: Scientific Enquiry
Investigative Skills

P-Level	Intended Learning Outcomes	Experiences and Activities for Investigative Skills	Assessment Opportunities

3(ii)	**Initiate**
	
	 • with a range of multi-sensory stimuli in a scientific context
		Facilitated through learning activities which include the above, as well as activities which provide opportunities to…
		
		 • search: surroundings for an item to manually/visually/bodily explore; for a known item hidden in a box such as own cup hidden amongst polystyrene chips; for someone to give an unwanted item to or to request an item from
		 • purposefully investigate objects/features in the environment such as by: shaking boxes to find out if they are empty; emptying boxes to sort through items; sorting through materials to find ones which can be torn; smelling food before tasting
		 • use switches to access a range of appropriate scientific equipment such as buzzers or lights in a simple circuit
		 • use switches to access science related software on computer
		 • choose an object of reference to request an activity
			Within the scientific context pupil may demonstrate an ability to…
			
			 • anticipate known events, follow routines
			 • initiate interactions, activities
			 • actively explore objects/events for more extended periods
			 • take turns in shared activities
			 • use emerging conventional communication by…
			   i) greeting familiar people
			   ii) attempting to sign
			   iii) using symbols
			   iv) recognising photographs
			   v) using objects of reference
			   vi) eye-pointing
			   vii) using PECS (Pictorial Exchange Communication System)

Science Key Stage: 2
Attainment Target 1: Scientific Enquiry
Investigative Skills

P-Level	Intended Learning Outcomes	Experiences and Activities for Investigative Skills	Assessment Opportunities
1(i)	**Encounter** ● a range of multi-sensory stimuli within a scientific context	*Facilitated through learning activities which provide experience of…* ● the sensory properties (smell, texture, visual aspects) of kinaesthetic reaction to familiar and unfamiliar objects such as: hair gel, shaving gel, cosmetics, speciality soaps ● the sensory properties of gases, liquids, and solids: ingredients used in cookery; solid and melted chocolate, solid and dissolved jelly; the experience of moving around wide-open spaces such as an almost empty playground and more confined spaces such as a crowded shop ● a variety of whole body movements including: rocking in a rocking chair; being bounced on a trampoline; travelling by train, boat or in a canoe ● a variety of temperatures through: the use of a temperature-controllable hand/foot spa; experience of food and drinks at different temperatures such as 'hot' chocolate and iced milk shake ● a variety of light intensities, colours and movement including: illuminated shop displays; arcade, computer and play station games; cinema and slide shows; pop videos downloaded onto computer; disco lights and lights in a photographic dark room; sensory room equipment such as bubble tubes, refractors	*Within the scientific context pupil is present and outwardly passive, participation is fully prompted.* Pupil may… ● make random involuntary movement, e.g. eye flicker ● show change in body tone ● show change in breathing rate/depth

Science Key Stage: 2
Attainment Target 1: Scientific Enquiry
Investigative Skills

P-Level	Intended Learning Outcomes	Experiences and Activities for Scientific Enquiry	Assessment Opportunities
1(ii)	**Awareness** • a range of multi-sensory stimuli within a scientific context	*Facilitated through learning activities which provide experience of the above, as well as activities which provide, within each sensory modality, similar/contrasting sensations such as...* • being touched on arms, legs, hands, feet, face with different textures, e.g. loofah, nail brush, sponge, make-up brush, shaving brush, battery shaver, hand lotion and massage rollers • being provided with different sounds to listen to; familiar people talking on the telephone, parent's voice played on personal stereo, computer generated voices, favourite songs played by different instruments on an electronic keyboard, environmental sounds; in a shop, railway station, in the countryside, park or woods, familiar songs in different languages, dialects	*Within the scientific context pupil shows reflex and intermittent reactions, emerging awareness, inconsistent and affective responses.* Pupil may... • tolerate a range of sensory stimulation: i) tactile ii) auditory iii) visual iv) gustatory v) olfactory vi) kinaesthetic

Science Key Stage: 2
Attainment Target 1: Scientific Enquiry
Investigative Skills

P-Level	Intended Learning Outcomes	Experiences and Activities for Scientific Enquiry	Assessment Opportunities
2(i)	**Respond/React** ● to a range of multi-sensory stimuli within a scientific context	*Facilitated through learning activities which include the above, as well as activities which provide opportunities to co-actively...* ● explore, using all available senses, objects with a range of similar/contrasting properties such as those linked to a hobby or leisure pursuit, e.g. gardening items such as plastic/clay pots, metal rake/wooden bessom, horticultural fleece/landscape fabric ● respond to the different smells/sounds/sights encountered when moving around a chemist shop, greengrocer, supermarket ● respond to the sensory properties of man-made and natural items including household items such as: metal and plastic cutlery, plastic and china crockery, metal and wooden cooking utensils, unprocessed fruit and vegetables and unprocessed cereals and grains, fresh herbs and spices (WARNING! Uncooked or hard food items are a choke hazard) ● respond to the effects produced when assisted to: operate cause and effect equipment via a switch such as massager, foot spa, music centre, radio, disco lights and when helped to produce effects in other ways such as roll a ball down a ramp or knock over table skittles ● respond to the start/finish of: a conversation/interaction with another person; the theme music of a favourite television programme	*Within the scientific context pupil shows interest.* Pupil may.... ● respond to the start/finish of proximal sensory stimulation ● respond to adult/peer interaction ● respond to start/finish of distal sensory stimulation ● begin to react consistently, indicative of a 'like' or 'don't like' response to given stimuli Pupil's response may be indicated by.... i) voluntary movement, e.g. change in facial expression, arm or leg movement ii) eye tracking iii) ear tracking (turns head) iv) vocalisation

Science Key Stage: 3
Attainment Target 1: Scientific Enquiry
Investigative Skills

P-Level	Intended Learning Outcomes	Experiences and Activities for Scientific Enquiry	Assessment Opportunities
2(ii)	**Proactive Co-operation** ● within a range of multi-sensory activities and with objects within a scientific context	*Facilitated through learning activities which include the above, as well as activities which provide opportunities to pro-actively…* ● co-operate in playing a range of age-appropriate games such as tug-of-war, skittles, boules (using a ramp if needed) ● assist, by giving differential responses, with sorting collections of items such as: real flowers from plastic ones, real fruit from wooden models, different personal hygiene products (shampoo, aftershave) with the same scent, e.g. 'Lynx' ● communicate preferences between: tastes and textures of unusual foods and drinks, different productions of the same sentence, e.g. when spoken through a voice changer, over the telephone, recorded, via the computer	*Within the scientific context pupil remembers learned responses and is pro-active.* Pupil may… ● glance alternately at two stimuli ● react consistently to the same stimuli ● express likes and dislikes consistently ● retain object momentarily without casting ● make general exploratory movements

Science Key Stage: 3
Attainment Target 1: Scientific Enquiry
Investigative Skills

P-Level	Intended Learning Outcomes	Experiences and Activities for Scientific Enquiry	Assessment Opportunities

3(i)	**Intentionally Participate**
	
	● with a range of multi-sensory stimuli within a scientific context
		Facilitated through learning activities which include the above, as well as activities which provide opportunities to…
		
		independently, using available senses, investigate their environment by:
		
		● observing, listening, tactilely exploring the immediate and distant environment: looking through foliage and moving into and out of dappled shade, listen/still when a new voice is heard, mix cookery ingredients by hand, squeeze damp soil, poke holes in clay, pull light cord to turn light on
		● accepting or rejecting: items to tear or crumple such as newspaper, bubble wrap, silver foil, card; food to eat or drink; different styles of music to move to
		● searching for: favourite items in a box, the switch when it is incorrectly positioned; the source of a friend's voice
			Within the scientific context pupil may demonstrate an ability to…
			
			● sustain concentration
			
			● display interested observation
			    i) focused looking
			    ii) focused listening
			    iii) reaching
			
			● communicate pre verbally using physical, vocal, auditory or visual skills by:
			    i) pointing to objects or events
			    ii) searching for an object after it has 'disappeared'
			    iii) searching for a stimulus after it has stopped
			    iv) choosing or refusing to participate
			    v) seeking attention
			
			● explore in more diverse way
			    i) rubs
			    ii) bangs
			    iii) pushes
			    iv) pulls
			    v) squeezes
			    vi) presses
			    vii) scans
			    viii) tracks

Science Key Stage: 3
Attainment Target 1: Scientific Enquiry
Investigative Skills

P-Level	Intended Learning Outcomes	Experiences and Activities for Scientific Enquiry	Assessment Opportunities

3(ii)	**Initiate**
	
	 • with a range of multi-sensory stimuli within a scientific context
		Facilitated through learning activities which include the above, as well as activities which provide opportunities to…
		
		 • initiate/continue adult or peer interactions
		 • operate switches for more extended periods to: use a blender to make a milkshake, sew a seam with an adapted sewing machine, listen to the whole of a song on the tape recorder
		 • communicate 'discoveries' when investigating different environments such as when on a mini-beast hunt, when pond-dipping, when exploring a park
		 • attend to objects/events for more extended periods; watch as powder paint is gradually added to water, as weights are added to test the strength of materials
		 • anticipate events such as a balloon bursting, getting splashed when an object is dropped into water, turn-taking in conversations
			Within the scientific context pupil may demonstrate an ability to…
			
			 • anticipate known events, follow routines
			
			 • initiate interactions, activities
			
			 • actively explore objects/events for more extended periods
			
			 • take turns in shared activities
			
			 • use emerging conventional communication by…
			   i) greeting familiar people
			   ii) attempting to sign
			   iii) using symbols
			   iv) recognising photographs
			   v) using objects of reference
			   vi) eye-pointing
			   vii) using PECS (Pictorial Exchange Communication System)

Appendix 1

School details

Langside School
Langside Avenue, Parkstone, Poole BH12 5BN
Tel: 01202 518635

Langside School (part of Dorset Scope's provision for people with special needs) is an independent day special school for pupils with physical and learning difficulties in the severe or profound range. A majority of the pupils have a language and communication difficulty and some have severe complex medical needs and/or sensory loss.

The curriculum reflects collaborative planning from a range of professionals including therapists all employed by the school to offer an holistic approach to education through individual education plans.

A recent OFSTED inspection highlighted that in the school 'teamwork makes an excellent contribution to pupils' learning' and 'relationships amongst staff and between staff and pupils are excellent'. It is within this culture and involvement in the community as a whole that our pupils reach their maximum academic potential and as high a level of independence and self-reliance as they are able.

Linwood School
Alma Road, Winton, Bournemouth BH9 1AJ
Tel/fax: 01202 525107

Linwood is an all-age range special school close to the centre of Bournemouth. We welcome pupils from a wide geographical area and support a comprehensive range of Special Educational Needs. The range includes pupils experiencing moderate, severe and profound learning difficulties.

Linwood, in common with all schools, is concerned with creating a learning environment that challenges its pupils with high expectations. We are also, however, in the privileged position of being able to acknowledge and respond to the needs of individual pupils with learning difficulties, their varying circumstances, stages of development and abilities.

As a special school, Linwood has, over recent years, increasingly become part of the main thrust of education. We are fully involved in the National Curriculum and offer the full range of subjects; pupils are involved in SATs for all Key Stages, we have responded positively to the Literacy Hour and Numeracy Strategy and we are involved with Baseline Assessment, as well as developing a comprehensive portfolio of external accreditation. The school has had an Outreach Policy for a number of years and staff have been supportive in other schools in a variety of ways. Linwood has recently been recognised as a centre of good practice in special education and has been awarded Beacon School status.

Montacute School
3 Canford Heath Road, Poole BH17 9NG
Tel: 01202 693239

Montacute School is an all-age foundation special school for children with severe, complex or profound and multiple learning difficulties. Some have additional sensory impairment, physical or medical needs, and others are on the autistic spectrum.

As a Beacon school, Montacute has a long tradition of curriculum development and a high quality range of specialist provision. The school is committed to multi-professional working, and the entitlement of all children to a rich and relevant education. Early Years and Post-16 groups are fully inclusive and, through carefully differentiated planning, all pupils with PMLD are enabled to access learning opportunities alongside their peers.

Mountjoy School
Flood Lane, Bridport, Dorset DT6 3QG
Tel: 01308 422250, Fax: 01308 458664

Mountjoy School is a small county mixed day special school for children and young people with severe, complex or profound and multiple learning difficulties. Some pupils have additional sensory and/or medical needs or have autistic spectrum disorders.

There are five classes at Mountjoy and transfer from one class to another is dependent not only on age, but also on a pupil's ability to gain maximum all-round benefit from the specialised teaching and learning approaches used within the class. Pupils with autistic spectrum disorders and those experiencing profound and multiple learning difficulties each have their own bases but any pupil may join another class for a particular subject if this is appropriate.

Pupils at Mountjoy School experience the full range of stimulating and often challenging experiences within the National and augmentative curriculums. Further details can be found on the school's website: www.mountjoy.dorset.sch.uk

Yewstock School
Honeymead Lane, Sturminster Newton, Dorset DT10 1EW
Tel: 01258 472796

Yewstock School is a Group 4 day special school based in Sturminster Newton in North Dorset. The school serves the whole of the north of the county, taking in the towns of Blandford, Gillingham, Shaftesbury and Sherborne as well as the more rural areas to the Somerset and Wiltshire borders. Pupils at Yewstock are aged between two and nineteen and can have a wide range of learning difficulties, including profound and complex, severe, or moderate needs as well as autistic spectrum disorders.

The school is fully inclusive at Nursery, KS 1 and Post-16. At KS 2 and beyond, pupils are linked by ability into parallel classes. Owing to changing needs this structure is currently under review.

Individual education plans

The first two examples of IEP's show how pupil information might be made accessible to staff so that they can help pupils work towards their short term targets, especially where pupils move between different learning environments in an inclusive setting.

Name:	Date of Birth: Year Group: Year 11 Class: Supported Learning Class

- Rett Syndrome.
- Immobile.
- Uses wheelchair.
- Gastrostomy fed.
- Scoliosis.
- Can eat orally, with caution.
- Requires resus trained personnel close at hand at all times.
- One-to-one carer (27.5 hours per week).
- Excellent at eye pointing.

Photograph of child located in this box

- Included with peers from Senior 3.
- Uses communication book.
- Is very much a young lady. Likes painting fingernails and hairstyles.
- Enjoys 'pop' music and looking at girls' magazines.
- Can choose to sit with friends.

Medical Equipment Used:	**Pastoral Care:**
- Wheelchair. - Leg gaiters. - Arm gaiters. - Chest jacket. - Wrist splint. - Box to sit on for posture. - Resuscitation equipment. - Gastrostomy tubes and pump.	- Respite care. - Works with Paediatric Physiotherapist twice weekly. - Works with Speech and Language Therapist weekly. - Review meetings with Orthotics for chest jacket and physio equipment. - Monitored closely by Paediatric Community Nursing Team. - Dietary requirements undertaken by registered Dietitian.

Date of Last Annual Review Meeting:
        4th June 2000

Date of Next Annual Review Meeting:
        4th July 2001

Name:	**Date of Birth:** **Year Group:** Year 11 **Class:** Supported Learning Class

- Microcephaly.
- Global developmental delay.
- Fully mobile with caution.
- Cataract in right eye.
- Limited vision in left eye.
- Soft diet.
- Weak left side.

Photograph of child located in this box

- Included with peers from Senior 3.
- Uses real object cue.
- Likes to row the boat with adult.
- With frustration uses Self Injurious Behaviour (diversion tactics will work)
- Does not look down, therefore will trip over objects.

Equipment Used:	**Pastoral Care:**
- Wedge for physio exercises. - Physio ball. - Shoe inserts fixed in situ. - Chair for inclusive activities, and mealtimes.	- Resides in a residential home. - Seen weekly by Speech and Language therapist. - Paediatric Physiotherapist writes physio programme. - Visits Orthotics.

Date of Last Annual Review Meeting:
4th June 2000

Date of Next Annual Review Meeting:
4th July 2001

Montacute School

Pupil's Name:

Term and Year: IEP Summer 2001

Curriculum Area	Key Targets	Delivery/Action	Outcome
Early Development English	To look at adult to confirm choice or question.	To be carried out at various times of the day. Questions such as 'do you want more?' have to be answered 'yes' by looking directly at the adult who is asking the question.	
Mathematics	Extend fingers with adult assistance to grasp and feel objects.	At various times of the day and during inclusive sessions, adult is to assist child in touching and feeling objects. Can also be carried out by some of child's closest friends.	
Physical	Sit on wooden box for 30 minutes daily to develop posture.	During appropriate times of the day in SLC, child is to be seated on the box and timed for 30 minutes. If she can sit for longer then do so. Best carried out in Supported Learning Class for safety reasons.	

Montacute School

Pupil's Name:

Term and Year: Summer 2001

Curriculum Area	Key Targets	Delivery/Action	Outcome
Early Development English	Reach out and grasp one item from a choice of two.	To be carried out at various times of the day. Hold up two real objects and say 'which one?' Encourage child to take the one he wants.	
English	Visually track an object that has been taken across his field of vision.	During various sessions at various times of the day take an object that attracts child's attention and slowly move it across his field of vision. This will encourage child to move his head and locate items.	
Physical	Independently walk up slope leading to Reception on a daily basis.	Take child for his daily mobility walk and habitually go up the slope leading to Reception. Allow child time to carry out this task independently. He can visit Leavers in the Flat as a reward and have a drink and something to eat.	

LINWOOD SCHOOL   **INDIVIDUAL EDUCATION PLAN**

Name: D.o.B: Class: Yr:

Teacher: Other staff involved:

Date started: **DATE OF REVIEW:**

STATEMENT NEEDS:	OTHER INFORMATION:

KEY OBJECTIVES	OUTCOMES/PROGRESS	DATE

LINWOOD SCHOOL   INDIVIDUAL EDUCATION PLAN

Name: Pupil A   D.o.B: Class: Unit   Yr: 5

Teacher: Other staff involved: JB, JN, JK

Date started: Feb. 2001   **DATE OF REVIEW:** Oct. 2001

STATEMENT NEEDS: Objectives:
To focus on appropriate sensory curriculum.
Access to N.C. at a level appropriate to her needs.
To develop – cause and effect.
       – an awareness of her environment.
       – communication for basic needs and expression of choice.
       – vocalisation for interaction.
To stimulate vision.

OTHER INFORMATION:
Weekly input from Physiotherapist.
Advice as appropriate from: S.A.L.T. O.T. Dietitian
   Teacher for V.I.   Teacher for the hearing impaired.
Advice and programmes received from the above are incorporated into Pupil A's timetable and inform the additional curriculum.
Pupil A's diet takes the form of prescribed fortified drinks.

KEY OBJECTIVES	OUTCOMES/PROGRESS	DATE
ENGLISH: Communication, Language and Literacy 1. To show response to the tactile vibrator when used during one-to-one communication activities. 2. To reciprocate interaction with an adult who is working in a one-to-one situation with her through touch. 3. To extend attention skills by using tactile stimuli in a distraction free environment. **MATHEMATICS:** 1. To develop an awareness of more by gently squeezing her right hand prior to repeating any action. 2. To locate and use a simple switch placed in a range of positions to gain a meaningful reward, e.g. a fan blowing air onto her. **ADDITIONAL CURRICULUM:** 1. To improve body control, maintain range of movement and encourage mobility, Pupil A needs: i. To stand daily in her prone standing frame for between 30 and 45 minutes. ii. To have a minimum of 30 minutes free play on the floor daily. iii. To use corrective seating at all times when seated. When using her class chair, she should wear her body brace. iv. To practise upright kneeling at her chest height whilst interacting with equipment for 10 minutes once a week.		

LINWOOD SCHOOL   **INDIVIDUAL EDUCATION PLAN**

Name: Pupil B   D.o.B: Class: Unit   Yr: 1

Teacher: Other staff involved: JB, JN, JK

Date started: Feb. 2001   **DATE OF REVIEW:** Oct. 2001

STATEMENT NEEDS:

To develop – Social awareness and awareness of his environment.
  – Self awareness through sensory stimulus.
  – Basic communication skills.
  – Self help and feeding skills.
Access to – Swimming and hydrotherapy.
Opportunities for occupational and physiotherapy practice.

OTHER INFORMATION:

Weekly input from Physiotherapist.
Requires two person lift.
Advice as appropriate from: S.A.L.T. O.T. Dietitian
  Teacher for V.I.

Advice and programmes received from the above are incorporated into Pupil B's timetable and inform the additional curriculum.

KEY OBJECTIVES	OUTCOMES/PROGRESS	DATE
ENGLISH: Communication, Language and Literacy 1. To locate a hand-puppet when introduced to his left side and track it to mid-line. 2. To follow the instruction,'Stretch out your arm.' 3. To use the 'Big Mac' switch to greet everybody during circle time when it is his turn. **MATHEMATICS:** 1. To demonstrate anticipation in relation to hearing the numbers 1,2,3. 2. To differentiate between likes and dislikes during assisted exploration of sensory stimuli. **ADDITIONAL CURRICULUM:** 1. To improve body control and maintain range of movement, Pupil B needs: i. To receive stretches to his hips prior to standing daily in his prone standing frame for between 30 and 45 minutes. ii. To work in prone on the Kirton wedge twice weekly. iii. To work in a side lying position twice weekly. iv. To use corrective seating at all times when seated. 2. To hold finger food and take it to his mouth. 3. To continue to practise reaching, grasping and holding skills.		

This IEP shows Medium Term targets. As the pupils is taught within a fully inclusive reception class, her objectives are set for all elements of English and Mathematics, and ICT is considered a cross-curricular core subject.

YEWSTOCK SCHOOL

Medium-term Individual Education Targets for January 2001 – January 2002

Name: Molly

English

1. Speaking and listening

Molly will demonstrate an understanding at a one word level, in context (i.e. music, stand, sit, names of familiar adults).
Molly will use vocalisations, to which an adult will respond and/or imitate.
Molly will work on identifying familiar photographs (family, peers and activities).
Molly will engage in early non-verbal communication (using Intensive Interaction).

2. Reading

Molly will share interactive books , by turn taking to lift flaps, turning pages, pressing sound makers, feeling material, etc.
Molly will continue to develop her pre-reading skills through the use of songs and rhymes, by showing anticipation using props, etc.

3. Writing

Molly will hold a marker pen to make marks on an outline drawing.
Molly will explore a variety of media with her fingers (i.e. scribbling in cornflour and water, shaving foam, etc).

Maths

1. Using and applying

Molly will use concepts learnt in Maths and generalise them in functional situations (i.e. make a choice from two objects, anticipate actions).
Molly will develop her relational play skills (i.e. using inset puzzles, building with bricks, container play, using tools, etc).

2. Number

Molly will participate in number songs and rhymes.
Molly will indicate that she wants 'more' or an activity to be repeated.

3. Shape, space, and measures

Molly will post shapes into a container.
Molly will anticipate routine daily events using objects of reference.

Science

Molly will participate in activities which explore scientific principles such as: light, energy, magnetism, etc., at an exploratory/sensory level.
Molly will participate in scientific activities related to termly topics, including: Light, Life and Living Things, Materials and Their Properties, Forces, Air, etc.

ICT

Molly will press a 'Jelly Bean' switch to operate the computer to build a picture which animates and/or a sensory display.
Molly will attend to the screen to watch animated stories, e.g. PB Bear.

Personal and social development

Molly will explore a variety of sensory stimuli (to include touch, smell, auditory, visual, kinesthetics, and taste).
Molly will respond appropriately to different environments (i.e. reach out to feel a display).
Molly will raise a spoon to her mouth to feed herself independently.
Molly will anticipate being changed when she is shown her nappy.

Physical

Molly will develop: strength, skill and co-ordination through her Physiotherapy programme.
Molly will stand daily in a Talia standing frame, for 45 minutes.
Molly will practise fine motor co-ordination tasks, including hand/ eye co-ordination.

MOUNTJOY SCHOOL

WEEKLY AIMS: TOWARDS MEDIUM TERM OBJECTIVES & SUBJECT AIMS

WILLIAM.....................................   ....Term 2001

Week beginning and Aim	MON	TUES	WED	THURS	FRI
14/9 IEP Communication skills When someone is working with me and they say my name, I will look at them. (Verbal prompts if needed)	✗	✗	✗	✓	✓
21/9 IEP Communication skills When someone is working with me and they say my name, I will look at them. (Verbal prompts if needed. To be achieved frequently*)	✗	✗	✓	✓	✓
28/9 English – signing I will co-operate with the task of 'signing' (fingerprint) my name. Hand on hand prompt, to isolate finger and press onto pad and paper. To be achieved frequently*	✓	AB	✓	✓	✓
5/10 IEP ICT When I have pressed the Big Red Switch I notice (head up, still, look) that the flashing light is working. Use of switch random place on tray in easy reach. To be mastered.	✗	✗	✗	✗	✓
12/10 IEP ICT When I have pressed the Big Red Switch I notice (head up, still, look) that the fan is blowing. To be mastered.	✓	✓	✗	✓	✓

*frequently = achieved 80% of time   mastered = 95% of time

Name: **IEP** **Term:** Spring 2001

	Weeks 1–2	Weeks 3–4	Weeks 5–6	Weeks 7–8	Weeks 9–10	Weeks 11–12
Physiotherapy: Unsupported sitting on box or stool, Use David Hart walker Standing without gaiters for changing.	For break and hand skills Daily use	For break and hand skills Daily use	For break and hand skills Daily use	For break and hand skills Daily use	For break and hand skills Daily use	For break and hand skills Daily use
OT: Use jelly bean switches Track objects 20cm from face.	NLS and ICT NLS	NLS and ICT NLS or NNS	NLS, Technology and ICT NLS or NNS	NLS, Technology and ICT NLS or NNS	NLS, Technology and ICT NLS or NNS	NLS, Technology and ICT NLS or NNS
Speech Therapy: Develop choice making with 3 flavours of drinks using smell.	PSHE	PSHE	PSHE	PSHE	PSHE	PSHE
Literacy: Use Big Mac to participate in stories Visual tracking of objects for activities	NLS	NLS	NLS	NLS	NLS	NLS
Numeracy: Domara sorting skills using hands to feel and show recognition of objects.	numeracy	numeracy	numeracy	numeracy	numeracy	numeracy
PSHE: Be dry & in pants all day	Am	Am	Am	Am	Am	Am
Use left hand on cup Hold spoon for 5 mouthful herself	Break Lunch daily	Break Lunch daily	Break Lunch daily	Break Lunch daily	Break Lunch daily	Break Lunch daily

References

ACCAC (1999) *Practical Suggestions for Assessing Pupils Working Towards Level 1*. Cardiff: Qualifications, Curriculum and Assessment Authority for Wales.

Ainscow, M., Hopkins, D., Southworth, G. and West, M. (1996) *Creating the Conditions for School Improvement*. London: David Fulton.

Aitken, S. And Buultjens, M. (1992) *Vision for Doing*. Edinburgh: Moray House Publications.

Ashdown, R. (2001) 'Design and technology', in B. Carpenter, R. Ashdown and K. Bovair (eds) *Enabling Access: Effective Teaching and Learning for Pupils with Learning Difficulties*. London: David Fulton.

Babbage, R., Byers, R. and Redding, H. (1999) *Approaches to Teaching and Learning: Including Pupils with Learning Difficulties*. London: David Fulton Publishers.

Brennan, W. (1985) *Curriculum for Very Special Learners*. Milton Keynes: Open University Press.

Brennan, W. (1985) *Curriculum for Special Needs*. Milton Keynes: Open University Press.

Brown, E. (1996) *Religious Education for All*. London: David Fulton Publishers.

Byers, R. (1996) 'Classroom processes' in Carpenter, B., Ashdown, R. and Bovair, K. (eds) *Enabling Access – effective teaching and learning for pupils with learning difficulties*. London: David Fulton Publishers.

Byers, R. (1998) 'Personal and social development for pupils with learning difficulties', in Tilstone, C., Florian, L. and Rose, R. (eds) *Promoting Inclusive Practice*. London: Routledge.

Byers, R. and Rose, R. (1996) *Planning the Curriculum for Pupils with Special Educational Needs – a practical guide*. London: David Fulton Publishers.

Carlton, S. (1993) *The Other Side of Autism: A Positive Approach*. Worcester: Self Publishing Association.

Cavigioli, O. (1997) 'Making it work' in *Special Children* October 1997, 15–18.

Coupe O'Kane, J. and Goldbart, J. (1998) *Communication Before Speech*. London: David Fulton Publishers.

Dessent, T. (1987) *Making the Ordinary School Special*. Lewes: Falmer Press.

DFE (1994) *The Code of Practice for the identification and Assessment of Special Educational Needs*. London: HMSO.

DFE (1996) *The Education Act 1996*. London: HMSO.

DfEE (1997) *Excellence for all Children: Meeting Special Educational Needs*. London: DfEE.

DfEE/DENI (1997) *Targets for our Future*. Suffolk: DfEE.

DfEE (1998a) *A Programme for Action: Meeting Special Educational Needs*.

London: DfEE.

DfEE (1998b) *Supporting the Target Setting Process.* London: DfEE.

DfEE (1998c) *Target Setting in Schools,* Circular 11/98 (1 July 1998). London: DfEE.

DfEE (1999) *Primary Education 1994–98: A Review of Primary Schools in England.* London: DfEE.

DfEE/QCA (1999) *The National Curriculum.* London: DfEE and QCA.

DfEE (2000) *Consultation Paper on School Target Setting Arrangements for Children with Special Educational Needs.* London: DfEE.

DfEE/QCA (2001) *Planning Teaching and Assessing the Curriculum for Pupils with Learning Difficulties.* (General Guidelines). London: QCA.

DfEE/QCA (2001) *Supporting the Target Setting Process: guidance for effective target setting for pupils with educational needs* London: HMSO.

DfES (2001) *Inclusive Schooling: Children with Special Educational Needs.* London: DFES.

DfES (November 2001) Special Educational Needs *Code of Practice.* London: HMSO.

Dearing, R. (1996) *Review of Qualifications for 16–19 Year Olds – Summary Report.* London: SCAA.

Fletcher-Campbell, F. and Lee, B. (1995) *Small Steps of Progress in the National Curriculum – final report.* Slough: NFER.

Hegarty, S. (1988) *Meeting Special Needs in Ordinary Schools.* Windsor: NFER-Nelson.

Lacey, P. and Lomas, J. (1993) *Support Services and the Curriculum – a practical guide to collaboration.* London: David Fulton Publishers.

Lacey, P. and Ouvry, C. (1998) *People with Profound and Multiple Learning Difficulties.* London: David Fulton Publishers.

Lawson, H. (1998) *Practical Record Keeping – development and resource material for staff working with pupils with special educational needs.* London: David Fulton Publishers.

McInnes, J. and Treffry, J. (1982*) Deaf-Blind Infants and Children – a developmental guide.* Buckingham: Open University Press.

National Curriculum Council (NCC) (1990) *Curriculum Guidance 3: The Whole Curriculum.* York: NCC.

Nind, H. and Hewett, D. (1994) *Access to Communication – developing the basics of communication with people with severe learning difficulties through Intensive Interaction.* London: David Fulton Publishers.

OFSTED (1995) *Guidance on the Inspection of Special Schools.* London: HMSO.

OFSTED (1996) *Setting Targets to Raise Standards: A Survey of Good Practice.* London: DfEE.

OFSTED (1999) *Special Education 1994–98: A review of Special Schools, Secure Units and Pupil Referral Units in England.* London: HMSO.

Ouvry, C. and Saunders, S. (1996) 'Pupils with profound and multiple learning difficulties' in Carpenter, B., Ashdown, R. and Bovair, K.(eds) *Enabling Access – effective teaching and learning for pupils with learning difficulties.* London: David Fulton Publishers.

QCA/DfEE (2001) *Planning, Teaching and Assessing the Curriculum for Pupils with Learning Difficulties.* London: QCA.

Ramjhun, A. (1995) *Implementing the Code of Practice for Children with Special Educational Needs.* London: HMSO.

SCAA (1995) *Planning the Curriculum at Key Stages 1 and 2*. London: SCAA.

SCAA (1996a) *Planning the Curriculum for Pupils with Profound and Multiple Learning Difficulties*. London: SCAA.

SCAA (1996b) *Assessment, Recording and Accreditation of Achievement for Pupils with Learning Difficulties – discussion paper no.7*. London: SCAA.

Tilstone, C. and Barry, C. 'Advocacy and Empowerment: what does it mean for pupils and people with PMLD?' in Lacey, P. and Ouvry, C. (eds.) (1998) *People with Profound and Multiple Learning Difficulties*. London: David Fulton Publishers.

Tilstone, C., Florian, L. and Rose, R. (eds) (1998) *Promoting Inclusive Practice*. London: Routledge.

Uzgiris, I. and Hunt, J. (1975) *Assessment in Infancy: ordinal scales of infant development*. Urbana: University of Illinois Press.

Ware, J. (ed.) (1994) *Educating Children with Profound and Multiple Learning Difficulties*. London: David Fulton Publishers.

Ware, J. (1996) *Creating a Responsive Environment for People with Profound and Multiple Learning Difficulties*. London: David Fulton Publishers.

Index